Beyond 17: The Apollo Applications Program and Losing the New Frontier

Fairleigh Brooks

Published by Fairleigh Brooks, 2023.

Table of Contents

Also by Fairleigh Brooks

Fiction

Notes of a Would-Be Astronaut

Beyond 17

**The Apollo Applications Program
and Losing the New Frontier**
by Fairleigh Brooks

To Lisa

A being from a higher plane sent to help navigate this world with me

Abbreviations

AAP – Apollo Applications Program
AES – Apollo Extension Systems
ALSS – Apollo Logistics Support System
ASTP – Apollo Soyuz Test Project
ATM – Apollo Telescope Mount
CM – Command Module
CORE – Congress of Racial Equality
CSM – Command Service Module
DA – Direct Ascent
EOR – Earth Orbit Rendezvous
EVA – Extravehicular Activity
IPP – Integrated Program Plan
ISS – International Space Station
JPL – Jet Propulsion Laboratory
LASS – Lunar Application of a Spent S-IVB Stage
LM – Lunar Module
LEO – Low Earth Orbit
LESA – Lunar Exploration System for Apollo
LFU – Lunar Flying Unit
LOR – Lunar Orbit Rendezvous
LPM – Lunar Payload Module
LRV – Lunar Roving Vehicle
MDA – Multiple Docking Adapter
SAA – Saturn Apollo Applications
SM – Service Module
SEI – Space Exploration Initiative
STG – Space Task Group

VAB – Vehicle Assembly Building

Preface

For many, another book about America in space, about the Apollo program, is as forgettable as another book about World War II or the Titanic or the Jazz Age. Ancient history, might as well be. Sort of de facto ruins, really, pyramidic in nature.

A significant number of people continue to believe Apollo was a hoax, a performance on a soundstage. Even during the time of Apollo few had an understanding beyond the most cursory of the monumental nature of what was accomplished in a very short time. Today that few is even fewer. I found myself writing this book, then, in an effort to provide some small facet of Apollo history and the times of Apollo.[1]

For homo sapiens, anyway, the time that is yet to be is always at hand along two possible vectors. There's the future, which is simply the turning of calendar pages, a succession of new dawns and dusks. This time yet to be is the same future experienced by our lesser cousins, the more intelligent of which might be vaguely aware that sunrises and sunsets and moon phases appear with regularity, acting as natural calendars.

And then there is The Future, which is imagined into gossamer existence, and then wrought into physical reality, and then dragged into the cultural lives within those calendar pages, except now tomorrow will be different from today. Or can be. This vector is open only to the hairless ape.

Across 300,000 years the physical articulation of our hands – wired so elegantly to the brainstuff of imagination – has allowed for what is imagined to be wrought. For better and for worse The Future has created vibrant, ever-changing cultures.

For better and for worse The Future has altered the face and the dynamic systems of Earth, our home.

Both the future and The Future, however, were bound by Newton's apple. The kept flame began denying the night long, long ago, and that light was perhaps the beginning of civilization. Many millennia later, in the early years of the twentieth century, the wrought reality of human flight denied in earnest (if temporarily) Newton's certainty, and so a sort of The Future 2.0 emerged. For a brief time in the 1960s in America The Future 2.0 was available for grasping. Imaginatively and technologically our grasp was equal to our reach. Culturally and politically it was not.

After determining the basic structure of this work as first envisioned, an account of the Apollo Applications Program and the state of politics and culture that held its beginnings, and then after beginning the body of the work, I came to realize an additional facet. I would also be writing both an homage to and a lament for the New Frontier, John Kennedy's view and hope for an American, and perhaps a global, modernity. This view, expressed explicitly in Kennedy's speech accepting his candidacy for president, was an undercurrent across the Apollo years.

The result of gaining a prospect on the New Frontier is the distinct, un-segued Part II of this book. Not typical for this type of work, this second part is largely a personal essay, and so is very often subjective. It may strike some as not in keeping with my initial stated purpose.

However, from my perspective the essay approach, and its subjectivity, best suited this goal, simply because I lived those Apollo years, growing from a small boy into an older teenager along the way. I was seven, sitting in my elementary school classroom, when I watched Alan Shepard lift off. At fifteen my understanding and accommodating parents took me to Florida to watch Apollo 11 lift off. I had just turned nineteen when the last Apollo flight, 17, landed on the moon.

On July 16, 1969, as I watched Apollo 11 launch, I trembled. Not out of an active fear of the report from the five huge F-1 first-stage engines and the resultant rolling thunder that engulfed the crowd, but from excitement. Surely, I thought, I was witnessing humanity step into an entirely new world, into The Future. However viscerally perceived at fifteen, this new world would be one not only of space exploration, but also one of enlightenment, equality, and technological wisdom. At that moment I fully expected to one day vacation on the moon. But then, what the hell did I know? I was fifteen, unwise to the ways of the world and the wiles of politics. Still, on that bright summer morning few wanted a fruition of the New Frontier more than I.

Fairleigh Brooks
March, 2023

Introduction

On December 19, 1972, the command module (CM) of Apollo 17 splashed down in the South Pacific. For most in the United States, including in Congress, and for those around the world the event was seen as the completion of the Apollo program, begun in 1961. Inarguably and in point of fact, Apollo was over, although the completion was de facto. Apollo, after all, wasn't completed. It was simply discontinued. Some might say killed.

The original Apollo flight docket included missions 18, 19, and 20. By 1970 those missions had been cancelled, even though the hardware, to varying stages, was built. Even if mission 20 had flown it would not have ended the program, not as Apollo was envisioned from NASA's point of view in the early to mid-1960s. That point of view saw Apollo as the start of a continuing quest, a quest without a prescribed end point.

That end point emerged anyway for many reasons. The war in Vietnam was an increasing drain on the treasury, as was President Lyndon Johnson's Great Society program. Civil unrest, both political and racial, demanded attention. Congress, populated significantly by people with mindsets from the 19th century, was largely uninterested in space exploration, in particular manned space exploration. President Richard Nixon, recently reelected for a second term, saw no political capital in such undertakings. Just as important, the general public was apathetic about Apollo by 1972.

Public interest in Apollo was intense in 1969, of course, as Apollo 11 landed the first two men on the lunar surface.

Interest was rekindled the following April by the drama of Apollo 13, which suffered an inflight explosion during the outbound leg. By ingenuity and luck, the three crew members returned safely to Earth.

After Apollo 13 public interest declined sharply, to the extent that the major events of Apollo 17 were not covered live by television. NBC, CBS, and ABC had received complaints about preempted soaps and game shows, enough to make the networks turn their backs on the public good and the obligation they had by use of the airwaves.[2]

Ironically, Apollo 17 was the first mission with an expanded scientific agenda. It was the third mission to utilize the lunar rover, from which live television pictures, now in color, were beamed to the CM in lunar orbit, then relayed to Earth. However, such history in the making could not compete with *Let's Make a Deal* and *Days of Our Lives*.[3]

And so Apollo 17 was indeed the end of Apollo, which, like a low-rated television show, failed to capture the imaginations of enough of us. Or perhaps failed, in the utter audacity of the pursuit, to deliver the mendacity the masses apparently wanted. Or needed. Who knows.

Since December 1972 no further humans have been true spacefarers, defined here as a person who has been caught in the gravitational field of another heavenly body. That number remains at twenty-four. No human since that now long-ago December has attained an altitude beyond 400 miles, much less beyond Earth orbit.

Throughout most of the 1960s the view of Apollo was unended. Missions 18, 19, and 20 were all scheduled for 1972.

BEYOND 17: THE APOLLO APPLICATIONS PROGRAM AND LOSING THE NEW FRONTIER

The Apollo 1 fire in January of 1967 and the Apollo 13 explosion in April of 1970, and the subsequent investigations of those events, each halted Apollo flights for significant periods and so slowed the program, resulting in Apollo 17 flying in about the same time frame Apollo 20 would have.

After Apollo 20 the Apollo missions were to have become longer, eventually lasting six months. An ever-expanding lunar base would have been started. Many other goals were to be pursued, including a manned flyby of Venus, and eventually a manned Mars mission in the mid-1980s. These further reaches into human curiosity, into a fundamental facet of what being human is, were called the Apollo Applications Program.

We have been given the scientific knowledge, the technical ability, and the materials to pursue the exploration of the universe. To ignore these great resources would be a corruption of a God-given ability.

– Wernher von Braun

PART 1

*The Apollo Years
and the Apollo Applications Program*

1

In the spring of 1961 John F. Kennedy was in the early months of his new administration. At forty-three he was the youngest elected president in United States history. The previous November he defeated Republican opponent Richard Nixon by a slim margin. Many of his detractors considered him brash, while many of his supporters were expecting greatness from this forward-looking new president.

After the January 20 inauguration, not three months passed before Kennedy found his administration, and himself, in a tight spot brought about by two events set in motion by Kennedy's predecessor, Dwight Eisenhower.

On April 12, 1961 Yuri Gagarin, a Soviet cosmonaut, became the first human in space. NASA's Mercury program hoped to launch Alan Shepard first, but technical and managerial delays postponed Shepard's launch many times. Shepard was finally launched in his Freedom 7 capsule on May 5.

Five days after Gagarin's flight, April 17, the Bay of Pigs invasion began, with the objective of deposing the revolutionary Fidel Castro as leader of Cuba. The plans for the invasion had gelled about one year earlier under Eisenhower. Kennedy was briefed days after his inauguration, signing off on the plan. The Mercury program also began under Eisenhower's watch.

Shepard's flight being second to Gagarin's was a predictable embarrassment. Regarding a presence in space, the United

States had been in a catch-up mode since the 1957 launch of the Soviet Sputnik satellite.

The Bay of Pigs invasion, however, was an unmitigated disaster. At first a military debacle, the event then quickly became a political failure for Kennedy, and an international humiliation for the nation. On the first day of the invasion Soviet leader Nikita Khrushchev threatened nuclear attack. Early in the invasion Kennedy scaled back air support to assuage international criticism. Although Kennedy's action was not cited specifically in a CIA report about the invasion issued seven months later, his decision was seen by some as a significant shortcoming.

Here, then, was a new, fresh president exactly three months in office when the Bay of Pigs invasion was halted. With two major defeats for the United States, Kennedy was now grasping for ways for the nation to attain some preeminence in the world regarding human advancement, particularly via science and technology. Many ideas emerged, including social engineering projects and medical triumphs. However, these such pursuits would not deliver results for many years, if not into decades.

Space exploration – manned space exploration – then emerged as the palette for this national display. And, really, this emergence was inevitable. Politically, and in the American public's perception, only one point mattered – Gagarin, a communist, had not only been first, he was also put into orbit. Shepard's flight was a suborbital ballistic flight.

Kennedy and his advisors considered the possibilities. Maybe an orbiting space station, or circumnavigating the moon. But the Soviets had more powerful rockets. They could lift more weight into space, into orbit. A similar United States capacity was years out. Kennedy decided to leapfrog the Soviets. What about going to the moon, landing a man on the moon? His science advisor, Jerome Wiesner, was against the idea, as were others advising Kennedy. Kennedy persisted, however. True, the United States, with a total of fifteen minutes of suborbital manned spaceflight, did not know just how this feat would be accomplished. But neither did the Soviets.

Adding to Kennedy's woes, soon after the Bay of Pigs invasion attempt ended the Congress of Racial Equality (CORE) activated the Freedom Ride, a challenge to segregation on Greyhound and Trailways bus routes in the South. On May 4, 1961 the buses, taking a circuitous route, left Washington, destination New Orleans. Although the riders encountered some incidents in North and South Carolina, they found no violent resistance.

However, on May 14, in Anniston, Alabama, on the road to Birmingham, and then in Birmingham proper, mobs of Ku Klux Klan members attacked riders with clubs and steel bars, injuring many riders quite severely. Buses were damaged, one set on fire. According to CORE director James Farmer, "We planned the Freedom Ride with the specific purpose of creating a crisis…. An international crisis, that was our strategy."

In late April, Farmer informed the offices of the president and the attorney general of the Freedom Ride. For reasons unknown, lower level agents failed to pass on the releases to both the White House and the attorney general's office. The violence in Alabama was a surprise to Kennedy.

Two weeks after the bus attacks Kennedy was scheduled to meet with top officials in Britain and France. By that time the world had seen images of American citizens attacked violently and mercilessly, and indeed gleefully, by other American citizens. Farmer had his international crisis, and now it was Kennedy's. Worse, on June 3 in Vienna, Kennedy had his first (and only) meeting with Khrushchev. The sixty-one-year-old premier sized up this younger man as the president who had botched the Bay of Pigs invasion. The meeting was a disaster for Kennedy.

Kennedy had already made his lunar landing address to Congress on May 25. We can surmise, perhaps, that the violence and hate inflicted on the Freedom Riders, and the weight of the crisis Kennedy carried with him to Europe, gave further resolve to his goal of depicting the United States as a forward-thinking, forward-moving nation.

Ingrained, historic racism juxtaposed with the moon journey – a journey at first simply imagined and then, with the scientific and technical ability to do so in place, emerging quickly –further illustrates the culturally seismic times from which Apollo rose.

In that May 25 speech to Congress, Kennedy proposed the United States land a man on the moon and return him safely before the decade was out. Kennedy was a skillful politician. His timing was spot on. Many in Congress were eager to close the gap between the two nations, specifically the missile gap but also the manned spaceflight gap. Enough members of Congress agreed with the proposal, and funding was provided quickly.

Of all the names associated with the U.S. space program, names such as James Webb or Wernher von Braun or Max Faget, to name only a few from a list of very many, perhaps the most important is John Kennedy. Von Braun was, of course, crucial to U.S. efforts. Faget was a brilliant designer. Webb, NASA's first director, had managerial and political skills that were equally as important. But as president, Kennedy was the gatekeeper, and he opened that gate. Kennedy was on many facets, but certainly not all, the man most responsible for July 20, 1969. He defied his advisors, moving ahead with the man-on-the-moon idea largely on his own. Most important, Kennedy imposed a deadline.

Although moon missions had been a realm of science fiction for many decades, and had been at least tangentially kicked around in the scientific and aerospace communities since about 1950, the idea of going to the moon emerged with some seriousness during the very late 1950s. At that time von Braun envisioned the mission as he had for many years. First building an orbiting space station, then building the spacecraft that would journey to the moon at the station, from which the craft would launch.

That late-1950s take gelled soon enough. By early October 1960, Apollo, at least as a preliminary plan, went from a serious idea to an accepted proposal. This was seven months before Kennedy's speech to Congress, and this preliminary plan envisioned the Earth-orbiting space station, followed by a circumlunar flight. A manned moon landing might then happen around 1975.

Kennedy's deadline proved crucial to Apollo. A span of fifteen years is and was a very long time in American politics. That span could have seen four different presidents and many changes in the House and the Senate. The Apollo program surviving politically during such a span was highly unlikely. The deadline removed Apollo from the usual process of approval, funding, and procurement, placing the program on a fast track, somewhat akin to the Manhattan Project.

Indeed, across only two years Congressional and popular support for Apollo fell significantly. By mid-1963 many in Congress and in the general populace were questioning the purpose and cost of Apollo. Kennedy was aware of that pulse, and that the cost of Apollo might stop the project.

In a September 1963 speech to the United Nations, with U.S.-Soviet relations having improved significantly since the 1962 Cuban Missile Crisis, Kennedy surprised not only the Kremlin but also many in Washington with a proposal for a joint U.S.-Soviet lunar landing project. There was outright skepticism in Washington since the Space Race – a race to be won decisively – was a key component of the administration's agenda. Although Soviet Foreign Minister Andrei Gromyko applauded the proposal, there was little to no further comment from either nation. Two months later Kennedy was dead, the proposal now moot and all but forgotten. Although uncomfortable to consider, Kennedy's assassination forestalled further opposition, to the extent that meeting the challenge of this gone president, and his deadline, was going to happen, period. However, by the late 1960s, and earlier on some facets, opposition to Apollo emerged again.

Apollo was expensive, but the cost was never unworkable, or outlandish as a percentage. NASA spending, for all programs, peaked in 1966 at 4.4% of the federal budget, then declined in roughly a straight line, reaching not quite 2% in 1970, about $3.8 billion. Since 1975, NASA's budget has been less than 1% of the federal budget, excepting 1991-1993, years in which NASA's budget was just over 1%. Since 2011, the budget has been right at 0.5% of the federal budget. As a comparison, the total cost of Apollo from 1961 to 1972 was $25.4 billion. The total cost of the Vietnam war from 1961-1975 was $141 billion, on average about $10 billion per year, with some years far more costly than others, especially around the culmination of Apollo. (From 1954-1975 the total cost in Vietnam was $168 billion.)

The costs of wars continue long after the wars end, requiring money that could have been spent elsewhere. Specifically, providing services to Vietnam veterans has been in the tens of billions per year since 1975, peaking at $25 billion in 2015, after which the effects of attrition became evident.

Still, landing a man on the moon was an easy target for those more interested in social programs, the environment, infrastructure, and fiscal conservatism. Congress declined to fund the Apollo Applications Program at a level that would have made the program viable. A few facets of the program, including Skylab and the joint Apollo-Soyuz mission, did come to fruition.

Over the decades since Apollo 17, and even before, was this question: Did a lunar-landing space race really exist between the United States and the Soviet Union? The answer, ultimately, was yes. Although Soviet posturing was in place in the late 1950s, concrete efforts towards a manned lunar landing did not follow immediately. The complete scope of the Soviet efforts was not known fully until the modern glasnost policy took effect in the late 1980s.

At the time John Kennedy addressed Congress with his moon landing challenge, Soviet leadership was well engaged in its posturing. In public statements the Soviet Union alluded to intentions of landing cosmonauts on the moon and establishing a lunar base. The public nature of these intentions faded quickly, however, and soon this aspect of Soviet manned missions was largely obscured by secrecy. The Soviets promoted their successful achievements, of course, but the events leading to those achievements were not transparent.

Sergei Korolev was the Soviet Union's von Braun. Like von Braun, Korolev was skilled in organization, long term planning, and design implementation. And like von Braun, he had thought about going to the moon long before Sputnik. He received permission from the Kremlin to begin pursuing such a mission, if preliminarily, in 1958, the same year Eisenhower approved the far simpler Mercury program.

After three embarrassing explosions of Juno I rockets early in the U.S. space program during the unmanned Explorer missions, then the U.S. space program, both manned and unmanned, was remarkably successful from Project Mercury on. Various unmanned missions, for example some Mariner and Ranger missions, experienced mission failure. But the Saturn V moon rocket, a hugely complicated, largely analog system of systems that all had to work in concert and in sequence, defied predictions and statistics with its success rate, which, across thirteen mission flights, was almost 100%.

Conversely, the Soviet program saw frequent failures after the initial success of Sputnik and follow-up Sputnik missions. The Luna missions ran from early 1959 to late 1970, when the last Luna mission, 16, returned a lunar sample to Earth. The failures occurred in various stages of specific missions. The Luna 2 mission impacted the moon, by design, on September

14, 1959, a first. A few weeks later, Luna 3 photographed the far side of the moon, another first. No one on Earth had ever seen images of the far side of the moon.

Luna missions 4 – 8 were intended to soft land on the moon, but all either missed the moon or crashed landed. Luna 9 soft landed successfully on February 3, 1966, transmitting both radio and television signals. The subsequent missions were successful. Overall, in addition to photographing the far side, and the first soft landing, the Luna program achieved a number of additional firsts – the first manmade object achieving escape velocity, and the first to deploy a rover. Luna 16's sample return mission was also a first.

By the time Luna 9 landed, Korolev had been dead three weeks, from complications after routine surgery. Korolev's death was a tremendous blow to the Soviet program.

The Soviet Lunokhod (Moonwalker) program was a lunar robotic craft intended initially to land before, and then support, a Soviet crew on the moon. The first Lunokhod mission (with nomenclature either Lunokhod 1A, or 0, or No. 201) failed soon after launch. Had the mission been successful, the rover would have landed on the moon in February 1969, about five months before Neil Armstrong's boot imprint. Lunokhod missions 1 and 2 were successful, landing on the moon November 10, 1970 and January 8, 1973. A third mission slated for 1977 was cancelled due to lack of a launch vehicle, and of funding.

And then, along with the death of Korolev, there was the N1 rocket, the Soviet equivalent of the Saturn V.

The Soviet Union, as they were posturing, considered Apollo to also be posturing on the part of the United States.

Despite the earlier nod Korolev received from the Kremlin, serious plans for a Soviet manned lunar mission did not begin until late 1964. In addition to this late start, the effort would be made with a small fraction the U.S. budget for construction and implementation, and with an even smaller research and development budget. The Soviets had no equivalent of NASA, no equivalent of James Webb, and were reliant on a military complex hostile to the very idea.

Beginning in October 1965, the N1 was rushed into production. The five-stage rocket had thirty mainstage engines. The three-stage Saturn V had five mainstage engines, complicated enough. The N1 would see a failure rate of 100% in four attempted launches, all unmanned. The second launch attempt, July 3, 1969, resulted in one of the largest non-nuclear explosions in history. The launching pad and surrounding facilities were destroyed completely. Before the launch thousands of personnel were ordered to evacuate the area. All remaining launch personnel were in bunkers. No fatalities were reported.[4]

Although a fifth attempt was scheduled for August 1974, the program was cancelled in May of that year. The Soviet Union was now out of the manned lunar landing business. (And so, by this date, was the United States.)[5]

But on July 3, 1969, as that N1 rocket exploded beyond spectacularly, many Americans, if to varying degrees of knowledge and sophistication, perceived that a continuing age of space would dawn in thirteen days when Apollo 11 launched. An age that would begin, that would be open-ended and expanding in purpose, and that would eventually take us with it.

2

At the beginning Apollo was, quite simply, a chess piece on the geopolitical gameboard. This point is beyond debate.

The launch of Sputnik on October 4, 1957 exposed a technological gap, both real and perceived, between the Soviet Union and Western nations, in particular the United States. Sputnik was the first manmade object placed into orbit. (The first manmade object into space was a V-2 rocket launched June 20, 1944.)

Many concluded that math and science education in the West had fallen behind such education in the Soviet Union. Although Dwight Eisenhower was not enthusiastic about manned spaceflight, he saw no choice but to respond to Soviet actions. Project Mercury was approved on October 7, 1958 during the second Eisenhower administration.

When John Kennedy was considering a milestone space feat, the extent of his administration's space policy was simply inheriting Project Mercury. As a senator, Kennedy had little interest in space exploration. Although he would become an enthusiastic supporter of Apollo, in the spring of 1961 he was simply looking to move his chess piece with determination. After Gagarin beating Shepard and after the Bay of Pigs disaster, Kennedy, like his predecessor, was compelled to act boldly and decisively, not only internationally but also domestically. Some among the John and Jane Does of America figured the Soviets, if they could orbit a spacecraft, would soon be able to drop atomic bombs on the United States from space, almost like tossing water balloons from an overpass onto the cars below.

Finding destiny in history is all too easy. Even casual students of history know that nothing was meant to be, that the outcome of an event in history wasn't baked into the beginning of that event. World events have been changed because the wind blew north one day instead of south, or because a messenger was captured, or arrived twelve hours too late.

There are many aspects of Apollo that might paint the program with destiny, if we let them. To begin, Nixon lost to Kennedy in 1960 by not many votes. Although speculative, as president Nixon probably would have finished Project Mercury and then gone no further.

Then, had the Bay of Pigs invasion been somehow successful, or never attempted, and had Shepard beat Gagarin – quite possible – Kennedy would not have found himself grasping at ways to promote the United States.

Still, all during Apollo, and before, serendipity did step in. The right man at the right time, such as James Webb becoming NASA administrator in 1961. When Webb's name emerged, over one dozen candidates had already turned the job down. Many in high positions didn't think Webb was right for the job. Webb himself was not too sure. And yet he was the right man. He was the perfect candidate, a skilled manager who, just as important (and at times more so), knew how to handle the politicians. In the early days of Apollo, James Webb was exactly the right man at exactly the right time.

Earlier, if Wernher von Braun had been captured by the Soviets after World War II, Apollo likely would not have happened. With Soviet troops just 100 miles from Peenemunde von Braun assembled his higher staff, asking among them to whom they would prefer to surrender. The consensus was not the Soviets. At that point von Braun and several hundred of his staff left Peenemunde in a scheme to find and surrender to American forces. Fearing the SS would destroy the results of their work, the men hid fourteen tons of documents in an abandoned mine.

The Apollo 1 fire, however, was a curious mix not only of serendipity, but perhaps of fate larger than beneficial happenstance.

When the Apollo 1 capsule was mated to the Saturn V rocket stack in January 1967, production of the CMs had become at times somewhat sloppy. Apollo 1 was scheduled to launch February 21. On January 27, the Apollo 1 capsule was undergoing a plugs-out test. This test was to determine if the capsule could operate on internal power, disconnected from the cables and umbilical hoses of the rocket stack. The test was also of voice communication between the crew and mission control, which was at times sketchy. There was to be no launch that day.

The fire was caused by a frayed wire, which sparked in the capsule's 100% oxygen environment, spreading quickly to the Velcro attached in many places inside the capsule. Had fire not ignited then, fire would likely have ignited during the actual Apollo 1 flight, or during a later mission. Given Congress's emerging diminishing support for Apollo, a fire during outbound or inbound flight would have almost certainly sunk the program. Even worse would have been a fire in the capsule while orbiting the moon. With two astronauts on the surface, that such fire would have left one astronaut dead immediately, while the two others could have done nothing but wait to asphyxiate, their bodies stranded – abandoned – on the moon.

Gus Grissom, Ed White, and Roger Chafee died, trapped in the capsule, but they died on Earth. Traditionally, we humans like to have a body. Returning the body of a loved or admired one to the soil of Earth, or using the body to further fuel a pyre, is a sort of unspoken agreement. Lament and regret and ruminative rethinking emerge when those we care about are lost at sea, be that sea of water or of a frigid vacuum. Such regret in both the popular and political spheres, with almost no doubt, would have been insurmountable. Like the later Apollo 13 explosion, the Apollo 1 fire halted the program for many months as a forensic investigation was conducted, and as portions of the Apollo capsule, particularly the hatch, were redesigned. The fire, then, likely saved the legacy of Apollo, to the extent Apollo would continue to happen.

In sharp irony, the fire happened just one day after George Mueller, director of NASA's Office of Manned Space Flight, held a press conference explaining and promoting AAP, which assumed an increasing NASA budget. Then, moving from one calendar day to only the very next, Apollo became permanently damaged in the eyes of Congress, and in much of public opinion. Congress would not – could not – pull the plug on Apollo wholesale, undermining the vision of an assassinated president, and branding the Apollo 1 crew as having died in vain. Still, Congress would let its rebuke be known, cutting NASA's budget. NASA's budget would continue to decline under the Nixon administration. Saturn rockets, by the dozens, had been key to AAP. In early 1970, Saturn production facilities were shut down permanently.

Still, Apollo moved ahead across the 1960s, even after the fire. By July 20, 1969, just eight years and fifty-six days after Kennedy's speech to Congress, Apollo had evolved well beyond that chess piece, into a kind of cathedral, really, the sort of holy place America builds.

Rocco Petrone, a key name in Apollo history, was a senior Apollo manager. A few years after Apollo Petrone said, "We've had a lot of reporting of how big the rocket is, how much noise it makes, pictures of guys on the moon. But what was the real meaning of Apollo? What did it symbolize? What were we after? For a few short years Apollo was almost like a Renaissance, but nobody wants to confront that sort of possibility now."

The continuation of that Renaissance-like time was once part of a vision of The Future, not simply the future.

3

All this world is heavy with the promise of greater things, and a day will come, one day in the unending succession of days, when beings, beings who are now latent in our thoughts and hidden in our loins, shall stand upon this earth as one stands upon a footstool, and shall laugh and reach their hands amidst the stars.

– H. G. Wells, 1902

Before the technology of spaceflight was dragged into reality, before that someday technology was imagined in earnest, before a human had the temerity to ponder such technology was even thinkable, there were people who looked up into the blue sky of day. Who looked up into the starry sky of night with a curiosity beyond astronomy and earthly navigation, and imagined breaking free of what Newton would later identify as gravity. Beginning with the wonder and envy of bird flight, but then going above and beyond. The sort of people then who, had they lived much later, would not have chosen *Let's Make a Deal* over watching humans walking on the moon.

In searching for seminal events that led eventually to 7-20-69, this wonder is found in ancient Greek mythology, in the tale of Icarus, circa 1700 BC. Icarus was the son of Daedalus. Daedalus was a master craftsman who built the Labyrinth for Minos, the king of Crete. In the Labyrinth was imprisoned the Minotaur, a man-bull monster.

After falling out of favor with King Minos, Daedalus was himself imprisoned in the Labyrinth. To escape Crete, Daedalus fashioned for himself and his son wings made of wax and feathers. Presciently, regarding modern aeronautics, Daedalus performed a test flight of his wings, defining their parameters. As their escape neared Daedalus cautioned his son strongly to follow his path in the sky, warning, "For the fogs about the earth would weigh you down and the blaze about the sun will melt your feathers." Earlier, and again presciently regarding spaceflight, Daedalus warned Icarus against both complacency and hubris.

However, his father's warnings could not leash Icarus's youth, and once discovering the exaltation of flight Icarus ignored the prime directive of test pilots, the overarching instruction meant to counter complacency and hubris – trust your instruments. In Icarus's case his instruments were the melting wax, and feathers falling away as he flew too close to the sun, until he flapped only his bare arms, plunging into the sea. The present day island of Icaria memorializes the fallen son of Daedalus.

Of course Daedalus's goal was to mimic bird flight, to get himself into the sky but not beyond. And his goal was escape, not exploration. But his son, even as he understood their escape, soon discovered that exploration was so close, to be had with a few vigorous wing flaps taking him upward still.

Although the envy of birds and the desire to gain their ability must be older than homo sapiens, there is a schism between once imagining atmospheric flight and imagining journeying beyond Earth's atmosphere and Earth's gravity. Until the mid-1800s or so pursuing leaving Earth as anything more than utter fantasy was simply laughable. For some the very idea was blasphemous. Then Jules Verne wrote *From the Earth to the Moon* in 1865, and *Around the Moon* in 1869. Although necessarily fantastic, his novels were not of fantasy but were science fiction. His ideas, extant and extrapolated, were based on well documented technology and hypotheses of the day.

The first flying manmade anything was likely a Chinese toy helicopter, basically feathers set at a lifting angle on a rotor spun between palms. Dates of its invention range from 400 BC to 320 AD. Around 1500, Da Vinci envisioned helicopters and designed an ornithopter, a machine that would, hypothetically, fly by mimicking bird flight.[6]

Across recent and not so recent history, then, lived people who imagined flight seriously enough to go beyond whimsy. Some acted on their imaginations by sketching devices that would have to await technologies and materials nonexistent in their day. Some tried to build their devices. Nearly all the device builders were modern-day versions of Daedalus and Icarus, mimicking bird flight.

Not until the Wright Brothers era did powered human flight, which is to say artificial flight, come to be. The Wrights, building on pioneering work by Otto Lilienthal, Octave Chanute, and many others, deconstructed bird flight into thrust, lift, and control surfaces. The resulting flight technology has never equaled the elegance of bird flight, but it has eclipsed completely the parameters of bird flight in speed, altitude, and distance.

On the one hand, rockets and airplanes are separate pursuits. Functioning rockets are much older than functioning airplanes. The first rocket dates to the Chinese Song dynasty around 1250 AD. Whereas modern rockets use gimbaled engines and limited aerodynamic surfaces for control, those very early rockets were only an expression of Newton's third law – they simply went skyward, period.

Even the Wright Brothers almost certainly wondered in 1903 (their first powered flight) what the limits of airplanes would be regarding speed, altitude, size, and application. Orville, who lived until 1948, saw part of that wondering answered, including the beginning years of jet aircraft. Still, he would have been astounded by the X-15 in 1959, a rocket-powered aircraft with stubby wings that could fly to the edge of space.

Airplanes, then, are not rockets. They require the fluidity of the atmosphere for lift and control, and they require oxygen for combustion. Still, as the twentieth century progressed airplanes and rockets, on certain facets, began a merging. The X-15 was emblematic of this merger. The aircraft was powered by a rocket engine using liquid oxygen, not a jet engine. It's wings were pretty much fins, somewhat like the sort that were on the bottom of the first Saturn V stage. Small rocket thrusters, like those on the CM, were used by the pilot to maintain stability and control. The life support systems on the X-15, including cabin integrity and a pressure suit for the pilot, had been developing along with jet aircraft across the whole of the 1950s. That evolution was applied directly to astronauts.

And so the dreamers, including those who became doers, have been around for centuries, the vast majority of their contemporaries utterly satisfied with the status quo, happy with their version of *Let's Make a Deal*, whatever that might have been. Cock fighting? Witch dunking? Burning blasphemers at the stake? Spectator leeching? Ah, good times. Pass the grog shots about to all! Let's, however, consider a few of the more recent dreamers.

Konstantin Tsiolkovsky (1857-1935) was born in Russia. By the mid-1880s, he had imagined space travel, addressed the practical means to pursue space travel, and had worked through the basic mathematics of rocket propulsion. He is considered the father of astronautics, although that field did not emerge specifically until the 1920s. He conceived of multistage rockets, liquid oxygen and hydrogen as fuel, space stations and space colonies. His ideas, theories, and direct research inspired Korolev as well as Valentin Glushko, another Soviet rocket designer and contemporary of Korolev, plus all those pursuing astronautics in any era. Tsiolkovsky's thinking and imagination was utterly remarkable for the time, a time in which the developed world still used horses for daily transportation and tallow, whale oil, and kerosene for lighting. A time when Darwin's theories were considered blasphemy by many, mere curiosities by most.

Robert Esnault-Pelterie (1881-1957) was initially a French aircraft designer. Inspired by the Wrights, he began experiments in gliders and then powered flight. A few years later he became interested in rocketry and space flight. Unaware of Tsiolkovsky, Esnault-Pelterie duplicated part of Tsiolkovsky's work. He is best known for *L'Astronautique* (Astronautics) published in 1930, and would go on to envision interplanetary travel and the application of nuclear energy for rocket propulsion. His work beyond aircraft was largely unnoticed by his countrymen.

Robert Goddard (1882-1945), American physicist and engineer, invented and fabricated the first liquid-fueled rocket, launching the rocket in 1926. His theories, research, and engineering made spaceflight possible, and he is considered the father of the Space Age. In 1919, the Smithsonian published Goddard's pioneering paper *A Method of Reaching Extreme Altitudes*, which details his experiments with solid-fueled rockets, his mathematics regarding rocket flight, and his theories of using rockets to explore beyond Earth's atmosphere.

Goddard was a reticent, private person, dismayed that his work was dismissed so handily in much of the physics community, and in the popular press. Despite Newton's third law, many figured a rocket's thrust would be inert in a vacuum. A *New York Times* editorial of 1920 mocked Goddard's space exploration ideas, stating Goddard lacked "... the knowledge ladled out in high schools daily." On July 17, 1969, one day after Apollo 11 launched, the *Times* ran a correction stating, "Further investigation and experimentation have confirmed the findings of Isaac Newton in the 17th century and it is now definitely established that a rocket can function in a vacuum as well as in an atmosphere. The *Times* regrets the error."

Hermann Oberth (1894-1989), German physicist and engineer, read and reread Jules Verne's *From the Earth to the Moon* and *Around the Moon* countless times, sparking his interest in rocketry at age eleven. His 1922 doctoral thesis on rocketry was rejected for being unrealistic and "Utopian." He published his thesis privately under the title *Die Rakete zu den Planetenräumen* (The Rocket Into Planetary Space), later expanding the work greatly under the title *Wege zur Raumschiffahrt* (Ways to Spaceflight). In 1953, he published

BEYOND 17: THE APOLLO APPLICATIONS PROGRAM AND LOSING THE NEW FRONTIER

Menschen im Weltraum (Mankind into Space), expounding his ideas for space-based telescopes, space stations, and pressure suits. During the 1950s Oberth would work for one of his former students, Wernher von Braun, in Huntsville.

Possibly the key word in the Wright Brothers legacy is deconstruction. Inherent to many dreams of humanity is deconstruction, the taking apart of natural human reality to reassemble in a new way, a view often forbidden by God and man for much of human history.

The very beginnings of a period, of an age, are often many decades before the age surfaces in the popular culture. As one example, in the case of our digital age those decades become centuries. In its most seminal form our digital age began in the early 1800s with the emergence of regional electric telegraphy. This notion was expressed more completely by 1851 with the completion of the transcontinental telegraph network, and the by then near universal use of Morse code, both of which opened the service easily to the individual user. Before the telegraph, the only way to deliver a precise message, in the exact words and syntax of the sender, was the way that had existed for millennia – a handwritten letter from the sender delivered physically to the recipient. Delivery beyond a region was measured in weeks, if not months. In the case of transoceanic delivery, the process might be measured in years.

The huge leap forward provided by telegraphy was to be found in, yes, deconstruction. Using Morse code, which simplified the transmitting process, precise messages could be carried across the nation using a binary system (not to be confused with digital) of signal or no signal; i.e., essentially ones and zeroes. Morse code deconstructed analog information into the binary information of dots and dashes, the point being that the meaning of the information was separate from the original form. That is, *Drive the cattle to the railhead* or *Uncle John is dead* had the same meaning to the recipient in the hand of the receiving telegraph operator as it would have in the original hand of the sender. Earlier, alphabets were a deconstruction of spoken language, the symbols representing specific, isolated sounds taken from the fluidity of language.

Even that Chinese toy helicopter from long ago was a result of deconstruction. A bird was deconstructed, if slightly, to have the feathers. Lift was deconstructed from the organic motion of bird wings, which involves twisting and warping in relation to the body, into a vertical shaft with angled feathers set at 90° to the shaft that push air downward, along with a delineated power source, in this case the rotation of the shaft provided by two palms moving each against the other.

Deconstruction, more broadly, is of course technology. Dreams must always wait for technology, simply because dreams come first. The visons of Tsiolkovsky, Esnault-Pelteire, Oberth, Goddard, von Braun, and Korolev, among many others, had to wait for theory and engineering to catch up, even as they were ridiculed by the John and Jane Does of their times.

The Saturn V, of course, was also a result of deconstruction/transformation. Lift and control surfaces were deconstructed into thrust and gimbaled engines. The unified V2 model was deconstructed into stages that were discarded as they were used. Natural oxygen was transformed from a gas into a liquid state. For the CM the visual navigation of old was deconstructed into data and the resultant algorithms (although sextants were onboard Apollo missions as backup).

BEYOND 17: THE APOLLO APPLICATIONS PROGRAM AND LOSING THE NEW FRONTIER

Perhaps first and foremost, in pursuing such concepts as the Saturn V, the human mind was deconstructed from a natural state (yes, perhaps a seamless state of idyllic heavenly grace and ease) into distinct realms of imagination and applied creativity, of hypothesis and theory, of art and science.

4

As alluded to in the previous chapter, an interesting aspect about the history of technologies is that the beginning of a given technology typically emerged many years, if not decades, before the technology became popularly known, or was available as a consumer product. Home video recording in cassette form, as one example, emerged in earnest in 1975 with the Sony Betamax, followed soon after by models from RCA, Panasonic, Toshiba, JVC, and Ampex. Some home recorders had been available since the mid-1960s, but they were very expensive, difficult to operate, had short recording times, and recorded in black-and-white only. Ampex produced the first videotape recorder for commercial television in 1956, almost two decades before the Betamax. Although not so much today, this pattern was once typical of consumer goods.

Rockets, in the public eye, also followed this pattern. In the United States the Redstone rocket, which boosted the first two Mercury flights, was the first rocket to receive continuing, wide-spread news coverage, becoming well known among the general populace. However, the Mercury Redstone was based on an evolution that started in the early 1950s.

The first Redstone was the PGM-11, first launched in 1953. The PGM-11 was a short-range ballistic missile. Variants named Jupiter-A, Jupiter-C, and Juno I followed. The Juno I rocket launched Explorer 1, the first U.S. satellite, January 31, 1958.

Still, the American public was already quite familiar with rockets by the time the Mercury Redstone hit front pages and national television news. True, these familiar rockets were closer to the starry visions of long wondered about manned space flight rather than the practical workhorses that emerged. Nevertheless, depictions in popular magazines and on television showing people venturing out into space captivated Americans for most of the 1950s.

These were not science fiction tales of the sort that ran in neighborhood movie theaters one after the other, many of them so cheesy you could have slapped one between two pieces of white bread and grilled up a sandwich. No, they were serious lay presentations to capture the imaginations of the American people. And they did. Similarly, as with technologies, the beginnings of cultural changes also typically emerge well before they are popularly noticed.

Wernher von Braun was a handsome, charismatic man who had an ability to connect with ordinary folks. The first five post-war years he was in the United States were spent in relative obscurity in Fort Bliss, near El Paso, Texas. Adjacent to Fort Bliss, in the New Mexico desert, sat the White Sands Proving Grounds. On these grounds, von Braun and his group test fired and improved confiscated German V-2 rockets brought over after World War II, the same rocket von Braun had developed at Peenemunde, the resort town on Germany's Baltic coast.

In 1950 von Braun and his Germans were transferred to Huntsville, Alabama. This group would help begin the Army's Ordnance Guided Missile Center, which today also includes the popular U.S. Space & Rocket Center. Huntsville offers a somewhat piney setting in the foothills of the Appalachians. Although the Germans arrived in Huntsville with preconceived notions about the American South – many true

– their new environs at least reminded them a little of Germany, certainly far more than had the baked and dusty Southwestern desert.

In early 1950 or so von Braun began a run of public speaking events. His talks about multistage rockets and orbiting space stations drew sporadic news coverage. Then in April 1951, von Braun was profiled in the *New Yorker.* In November, with that happenstance that would later seem to nudge the Apollo project in right directions, he crossed paths with a journalist. The journalist was Cornelius Ryan, known for his World war II military histories *The Longest Day*, *The Last Battle*, and *A Bridge Too Far.*

Ryan was working as an associate editor for *Collier's*, at the time a very popular general interest news weekly. He had been sent to cover an esoteric conference on space medicine. Von Braun was also in attendance.

How to report the conference, or what to even begin writing, was not forthcoming to Ryan. He retreated to the hotel bar. So did von Braun. The two men met, and talked over drinks. Von Braun offered his help, plus the help of two colleagues. The three sold Ryan on the idea of human space flight, on the notion that humans in space was all but a certainty. Inevitable, really, with the proper effort. And enough money.

The next March, *Collier's* began a now famous series of articles on humans in space, fully illustrated by Fred Freeman, Rolf Klep, and Chesley Bonestell. All were highly accomplished illustrators in the photorealistic style, but Bonestell came to the project as a legend in his field. (Any issue from the series is today highly collectible.) Of course, in

1952 *humans in space* meant men, specifically highly trained white men. But the allusion was that eventually *humans in space* would include you and me.[2]

As we stare today at our various screens, as we view our smart phones as simply a basic necessity, younger people, and even the not so young, might try to understand the state of technology and of daily life in 1952. Houses often had just one telephone, on a cord that came out of a wall. The handset alone was massive enough to be a murder weapon. Televisions had round picture tubes and black-and-white images with a resolution laughable today. In larger cities viewers had two, maybe three channels of programming that signed off at midnight. Only commercial buildings were air conditioned, and virtually no cars were. And in Huntsville, as in countless other locales, black was black and white was white. Period.

Consider that a fifty-five-year-old man or woman alive in 1952 was born in 1897. You know, horses and buggies, cowboys and Indians. Former slaves and Civil War veterans as relatives. Gas lighting still in places. Or kerosene. Telephones were just beginning to come into widespread use, and even then were a luxury for the better off. Many by the millions had grown up on farms without electricity or running water. In 1952 many of those far beyond cities still lacked electricity and municipal water, and telephones. The Wright Brothers' first brief flights had happened not fifty years earlier. And yet here, in *Collier's,* on page after page of full color illustrations amid compelling text was The Future, not simply the turning of calendar pages.

Of course The Future was already at hand in 1952. Television, automobiles, modern medicine, modern highways, routine airplane flights for anyone with the price of a ticket. Modern architecture. A few years later Elvis, and Nabokov's *Lolita.* And yet, leaving Earth was an altogether other sort of future. Not only impossible, but unimaginable, really, beyond its depiction in adolescent pulp science fiction. But now here's this German scientist who's telling us *Why not?* Telling us in perfect English with a German accent, which somehow made the impossible seem possible.

Then more.

In 1955 Disneyland opened in Anaheim, California. The opening was televised live on ABC.

Fourteen thousand were invited. Twenty-eight thousand showed up. The place was an immediate success. Inside the park was Adventureland and the Jungle Cruise and Sleeping Beauty's Castle. And Tomorrowland. Quoting Walt Disney when dedicating Tomorrowland, "Tomorrow can be a wonderful age. Our scientists today are opening the doors of the Space Age to achievements that will benefit our children and generations to come. The Tomorrowland attractions have been designed to give you an opportunity to participate in adventures that are a living blueprint of our future."

Tomorrowland included Rocket to the Moon, a simulated space flight to the moon. The biggest attraction was the TWA Moonliner, a seventy-six-feet-tall full-sized mockup of the classic cigar-shaped rocket that, from the 1955 perspective of the public, was the sort of craft that would be built at von Braun's orbiting space station. The rocket was designed principally by Disney employee John Hench, along with von Braun and German American rocket designer Willy Ley. (The TWA Moonliner was mostly for promoting the popular perception of manned spaceflight. It looked very little like the moon-bound, space-station-launched spacecraft von Braun had proposed a few years earlier. Those craft, since they would never fly in atmosphere, were basically unclad fuel tanks bolted to an exposed framework.)

The Moonliner had already appeared in prop form on the "Man in Space" episode of the *Walt Disney's Disneyland* television series. The episode aired originally on March 9, 1955.

"Man is Space," with von Braun often onscreen as narrator, was a serious depiction of what might lie ahead, say around 1985. Although the production looks a bit kitschy from today's CGI perspective, at the time Disney was using topnotch effects. That night about 40,000,000 people watched the episode, about 25% of the total U.S. population. The episode was nominated for Best Documentary Short at the Academy Awards.

From about 1957 on print advertising, in both trade and popular magazines, would push the man in space idea. Aerospace companies such as Lockheed, Convair, and Boeing advertised in the trades. Even NCR (National Cash Register) ran trade ads to highlight their keypunch machines, at a time when computers were programmed with punched cards. Other more mainstream and recognizable companies such as RCA, Westinghouse, and Goodyear advertised in the popular weekly or monthly magazines to highlight contributions the companies were making to the space race. Once again The Future in popular depiction was being created, and was just several years out.

TWA lent its logo to the Disney exhibit because, in however preliminary a way, the company honchos figured someday TWA would, paraphrasing Frank Sinatra, fly us to the moon.

Pan Am figured likewise. In the early production years of *2001: A Space Odyssey* Pan Am showed Stanley Kubrick the company's plans for a spaceliner. Kubrick thanked the company by placing the blue Pan Am logo on the spaceliner model in his film. From 1968 to 1971 Pan Am actually took reservations for the first Pan Am flight to the moon, although no departure date was given or implied. The airline issued "First Moon Flights Club" membership cards, numbered and signed by the vice president of sales.[8]

Soon after the beginning of Project Mercury, NASA, rather than simply delivering facts, provided to the press ready-to-print stories and photos, much like stories coming over the AP and UPI teletype feeds in newsrooms. NASA also worked closely with industry to create media pieces favorable to both. Unlike in the Soviet Union, the U.S. space program was out there, man, smack in the face of America. Go to space? Hell yes! Stay in space? Of course.

The 1950s and the early to mid-1960s were a time, for better or worse, of an almost unquestioned optimism in mainstream America, one not really knowable today. Many at NASA and in the aerospace industry, beyond their professional status, were also caught up in the optimism and ensuing enthusiasm that ran through the public imagination. Although the concepts and methods that did emerge, out of practicality, to get to the moon and back did not look much like the TWA Moonliner, or von Braun's vision of exposed fuel tanks, the underlying notion of bringing into reality what can be imagined and wrought and dragged continued.

5

None of Apollo, the part that did happen and the part that did not, would have or could have happened without the Saturn V. Before we explore the specifics of AAP, then, let's consider the Saturn V; what was actually launched to the moon by the rocket; and the assembly of the stages and payload. Oh, and then there was moving a 363-feet tall piece of hardware weighing 230 tons from the building in which it was assembled to the launch pad.

Kennedy's speech to Congress in May of 1961, with the goal of a manned moon landing before the decade was out, would eliminate von Braun's long-held vision of constructing an orbiting space station, at which a rocket to the moon would be constructed. This method would have required multiple launches of initial, smaller Saturn versions, the Saturn I and IB, to ferry up materials. The constructed moon rocket would have the advantage of starting from Earth orbit, already very significantly out of Earth's gravity well.

The orbiting space station soon enough became a pipe dream, and was really not needed for assembling a lunar spacecraft in orbit. Assembling without the station was called Earth Orbit Rendezvous (EOR). Early on, EOR was pretty much assumed, even as the practical details of assembling huge components in orbit remained both unknown and daunting. EOR still provided the gravity well advantage. Leaving from an orbital point was the same as leaving from a space station.

This initial vision of Von Braun's, and the resulting EOR, dealt with gravity in stages, thus allowing for the smaller rockets to deliver material and sections of the moon rocket into Earth orbit. A rocket departing from the space station – or from an EOR point – would have needed only enough fuel to reach the moon, land, and then launch from the moon and return to Earth in a splashdown. The word *only*, however, needs some qualifying. From Earth orbit the moon is still 240,000 miles distant, but all of the fuel needed for Apollo (the CSM and LM leaving from an EOR point) to go to the moon, land, take off, and return to Earth – all of that fuel being contained within the CSM and the LM – was a tiny fraction of the approximately 6,000,000 pounds of fuel burned in the three stages of the Saturn V over about eight minutes to reach orbital velocity. Getting out of Earth's gravity well required that huge amount of expended energy.

When Kennedy made his speech another option, direct ascent (DA), remained under consideration – sort of the TWA Rocket to the Moon from Tomorrowland becoming a reality, but not really. The TWA rocket going to and returning from the moon as one unified item was always science fiction, even when, early on, it was imagined popularly as the coming reality.

NASA's definition of direct ascent was notably different.[2]

In that definition the craft landing on the moon was unified. That craft would still be boosted into Earth orbit for trans-lunar injection using a three-stage rocket, but it would land on the moon as a fully self-contained cylindrical craft about as tall as the TWA rocket. Fully self-contained meant all rocket engines, fuel, pressurized crew quarters, life support, and equipment for exploring the moon in one craft for a seven-day stay. The top part of the craft, the equivalent of the

CSM, would launch from the moon. Compared to what did happen direct ascent was on a larger scale in all respects.

That larger scale would have needed a rocket far bigger than the Saturn I or IB, and bigger than the as yet unrealized Saturn V. A huge vehicle, slightly taller but significantly wider than the coming Saturn V, the Nova would have delivered 17,000,000 pounds of total thrust between three stages. The Saturn V delivered 9,300,000 pounds of total thrust between three stages.

Nova soon became both an engineering unlikelihood and what would probably be a logistical nightmare. Engineers weren't sure the thing could be launched from land, given the noise and vibration. Some considered launching the Nova from ocean-going barges. The Nova soon became unhinged as a concept, leaving EOR as the remaining method.

Still, Nova likely did serve a real purpose. The rocket pre-dated the Saturn V on the drafting table, and remained under consideration to an extent as the Saturn V was designed. As engineer Owen Maynard observed, had the huge Nova not been considered – more or less realistically – the Saturn V, even at two thirds scale to the Nova, would itself have seemed all but impossible.

However, another method would emerge, or re-emerge. Existing in theory since 1916, Lunar Orbit Rendezvous (LOR) won out over EOR, which now meant that the actual hardware to reach the moon, land on the moon, launch from the moon, and return to Earth had to be launched in one unified package from sea level, at the bottom of Earth's gravity well. (Although LOR sounds something like DA, it was not.) Whereas EOR would have utilized the initial Saturn rockets, and the once proposed Saturn C-3, now an expanded rocket, the Saturn V, was needed. The Saturn V was much larger than earlier versions, roughly twice the size of the Saturn I.[10]

The overriding factor in the Saturn V equation, and in the overall equation of any full Apollo mission, was fuel. Even the initial slide rule run throughs told LOR offered very significant fuel savings over both DA and EOR.

Consider. You're driving down the highway with the fuel needle on E. You pull into a gasoline station to fill the tank. Assuming a tank capacity of twenty gallons, when you leave the gasoline station your transportation system – your car, you, and any passengers and cargo – now weighs about 160 pounds more, the weight of the gasoline. Although not significantly, your mileage has decreased, because now a portion of the gasoline in the filled tank must be used to transport the gasoline itself.

This simple example, expanded exponentially, was fundamental to a rocket as big as the Saturn V. On the launch pad the fueled rocket weighed 3100 tons. As stated the unfueled rocket weighed 230 tons. Of the total tonnage, then, more than 90% was fuel, a large percentage of which was used to launch the fuel itself.

From the start engineers looked for any opportunity to reduce weight in every system that made up the Saturn V supersystem. For example, the basic bulkhead of the LM was designed as a single piece to avoid welds. Not that welds could not have withstood the rigors of spaceflight, but the line of a welded seam plus the two joined pieces of metal weighed more than the continuous section of metal without the seam. Pursuing the same weight-saving goal, lunar astronauts left behind tools and equipment, and even their own excrement, on the moon.

And of course, within the fuel equation, the best way to save fuel was to not use it. Just as an EOR-constructed spacecraft would have, the resultant outbound LOR Apollo spacecraft used Newton's third law to nearly maximum effect in the vacuum and relative weightlessness of space. Apollo 8, and Apollo 10 through 17 (Apollo 9 was a dress rehearsal in Earth orbit) largely coasted to the moon and to lunar orbit, after initial firing to reach Earth orbit, and then firing to reach escape velocity, plus scheduled burns enroute, and brief course-correcting burns. Those missions did not simply blaze along Buck Rogers style, flames roaring out the back all along, burning precious fuel.

The Saturn V with payload was 363 feet tall (excluding the escape tower). However, that payload – the parts going to the moon, the parts that would return to Earth's atmosphere, and the one part that would actually return to Earth whole – made up only the top twenty feet or so of the rocket stack on the launch pad. (Unseen were the CSM rocket nozzle, and the LM stored below the nozzle.) This method lacked the swashbuckling glint of a DA rocket, but by July of 1962 it was the only way to go. What LOR lacked in swashbuckling it gained in engineering elegance.

As noted, EOR was assumed early on. Although LOR emerged within NASA in 1958 as an alternative, the method was considered too dangerous, considering docking two independent spacecraft in space had not been achieved, even in low Earth orbit. (Docking experience would be gained with the Gemini project.) EOR remained first choice until late 1961.

In November 1961 Dr. John Houbolt, an aerospace engineer at Langley Research Center, began advocating for LOR, noting LOR was not only the most feasible way, it was the only way to meet Kennedy's deadline. He did not originate the idea, but over the previous eighteen months the elegance of LOR had become insistently clear to him.

Houbolt bucked the usual chain of superiors, writing a private letter directly to NASA administrator Robert Seamans. This action angered many within that chain, but eventually LOR, which offered not just significant fuel savings, but also an implicit simplification of the entire project, won out. James Webb approved LOR in July 1962. Thus was the Saturn V born.

Fuel was key to the LOR decision. And so another analogy, if you will. Let's say the bottom of the Grand Canyon has never been explored. And let's say satellite imagery has shown a natural soil and rock ramp that goes from the rim to the bottom at a more-or-less uniform angle, a freak geological anomaly. The decision is made to mount an exploratory expedition from Washington D.C. to the bottom of the canyon, explore, return to the rim and return to Washington. The expedition must leave Washington, explore the canyon and return to Washington as a single unit. No stopping along the way, no refueling, all supplies on board for a crew of three upon departure.

The DA version of this Grand Canyon expedition (in the original definition of DA, the TWA rocket) would have been a large motor home with auxiliary fuel tanks, with enough food and water on board to last seven days, and enough pounds of gasoline to reach the Grand Canyon, descend to the bottom, drive out, and drive back to Washington.

When the motorhome arrived at the rim, the driver would back the motorhome down the ramp. A very dicey move, but necessary. At the end of the expedition the motorhome would have to be headed up the ramp, then drive up the ramp to the rim to head home.

In the same way, the pilot of the EOR spacecraft, or of a direct ascent spacecraft, would have had to land a spacecraft maybe seventy-five feet tall tail first. With LOR, the LM also landed tail first. But the LM was only fourteen feet tall, and the pilot was standing, looking through downward-facing windows in the direction of descent.

But hold on, a Dr. Houbolt would have said. Instead of sending this large vehicle – all of it – all the way to the Grand Canyon and then to the bottom, then drive out of the canyon and drive all the way back to Washington, how about using an SUV, pulling a trailer holding a motorcycle? The SUV would need auxiliary fuel tanks, as would the motorcycle, but much less fuel would be needed to get this far less massive system from Washington to the rim of the Grand Canyon. At the rim two crew members would exit the SUV while the third stayed inside to monitor events and relay communication. The two would ride the motorcycle with the auxiliary gasoline tank off the trailer, then ride the motorcycle down the ramp to the bottom. After exploring they would fill the main gasoline tank from the auxiliary tank, then leave that tank at the bottom of the canyon. They would ride back up to the rim, then leave the motorcycle at the rim. They would then unhitch the trailer from the SUV, rejoin their lone crewmate, and head back for Washington in the SUV. This would have been the LOR version, leaving behind equipment no longer needed, reducing weight, and so fuel consumption, at each juncture.

The DA approach, in which the entire rocket package would have launched from Earth at sea level, then the actual lunar rocket travelling to the moon leaving from LEO, landing on the moon, the top part (CSM equivalent) launching from the moon, and returning to Earth in a splashdown, would have involved the "dead weight" aspect of fuel, in that the fuel to land the entire lunar spacecraft on the moon, including the CSM equivalent, and the fuel to launch the CSM equivalent out of the moon's gravity well, would have had to be taken to the lunar surface. This would have required larger, heavier fuel tanks, which would have required more pounds of fuel, and that extra fuel would have required even more fuel, and so on. The EOR approach – assembling the lunar spacecraft in Earth orbit – lessened the dead weight factor, but that factor was still very significant.

True, the dead weight aspect can also be seen as a factor with LOR, burning fuel for the purpose of moving fuel, but with LOR that factor was shifted mostly to the beginning of the flight, when fuel consumption was less of a variable, and when an emergency was addressable. Fuel consumption was much more of a factor regarding survival 240,000 miles from Earth.

As the Apollo 11 LM, *Eagle*, was in final approach to land on the moon a computer overload – indicated by the now famous 1202 code – caused the spacecraft to overshoot the original landing coordinates. Armstrong took manual control of the LM after observing Aldrin and he headed for a large crater surrounded by a boulder field. *Eagle* finally landed with fuel for about ten more seconds of burn time. In other words, *Eagle's* fuel needle was just about below E, and there was no Shell station on the moon selling rocket fuel.

The beauty of LOR was its system of components. Each component was disposed of after fulfilling its purpose, and so allowed for the best way to save fuel – by not using fuel. Contrasting with EOR and DA, as just one example the much larger unified spacecraft would have had to carry a larger heat shield (for reentering Earth's atmosphere) all the way to the moon and down to the bottom of the moon's gravity well, and so also carry the fuel to launch the weight of the heat shield off the moon. LOR also used a heat shield, but it remained in lunar orbit as an integral part of the command module. When astronauts launched from the moon they ascended in the top component of the LM, the ascent stage, which had its own rocket engine. The bottom component, which contained the descent engine, remained on the lunar surface. Before the command service module headed back to Earth the ascent component of the LM was jettisoned. On the moon today are seven LM descent components, and six LM ascent components, which, after being undocked from the command module, orbited the moon briefly before crashing into the regolith. The discrepancy involves Apollo 10, which was a full rehearsal in lunar orbit without landing. The Apollo 10 descent stage orbited and then crashed. The ascent stage was fired beyond the moon into a heliocentric orbit. In recent years, astronomers have tracked an object that appears, with a 98%

probability, to be the ascent stage. Also on the moon today are three lunar rovers.

The impetus for the Nova, and so the Saturn V, can be traced to the launch of Sputnik 1, October 4, 1957. Sputnik scared the pants off Western nations, particularly the United States. Post-war rocket development in the U.S., based on confiscated V2 rockets, had been steady but unspectacular. For the dozen or so years after arriving in the U.S. in 1945 Wernher von Braun's role was mostly as consultant to American engineers.

His role changed quickly with Sputnik. Von Braun now found himself again, happily, at a drafting table. His team soon developed the Juno I rocket, which launched Explorer 1, the first American satellite, February 1, 1958. Von Braun would view the Juno I as a seminal moment in Saturn V development.

As stated, three variations of Saturn rockets were built – Saturn I, Saturn IB, and the Saturn V. The proposed but never built Saturn C-3 would have been the principal go to rocket for EOR.

In January 1962, NASA announced plans to build the Saturn V. The rocket required more than five years of designing, testing, and fabrication, launching the first time November 9, 1967.

As an engineering feat the Saturn V is to be included with the pyramids at Giza, with Notre Dame or Chartres, with the Great Wall of China, or the Panama Canal. The rocket was indeed one of those cathedrals America builds, in this case an homage to the living and those who will live, not to the dead and the past. Yes, a creation to the ethereal, but a celestial ether, an outland that, by its very hostility and distance, was attainable only in The Future.

Statistically, Saturn V's success rate was beyond remarkable. It was phenomenal, exceeding the most optimistic expectations. The rocket sat at the opposite end of the scale from the 100% failure rate of the ill-fated Soviet N-1. In the early days of designing and planning the Saturn V NASA expected a failure rate as high as fifty percent.

The Saturn V flew thirteen times, eleven times with a crew. Those thirteen flights can't be given an actual 100% success rate, however. Apollo 6, the final uncrewed test flight, did have significant problems of pogoing and engine ignition, due to hydraulic resonance, plus a temporary partial vacuum in the firing chamber, as well as ruptured fuel lines. Although the flight more or less served its purpose, these problems gave pause to NASA engineers. And again the serendipity, considering the hydraulic resonance happened on an unmanned test flight, which offered the opportunity to address the resonance before Apollo 7, the first crewed flight. So, OK, not 100%, but 99% or so worked just fine.

The Vehicle Assembly Building

Cape Canaveral gained that name during Spanish colonial times, Cabo Cañaveral (reed bed) in the original Spanish. In November 1963, seven days after Kennedy's assassination, President Johnson, by executive order, renamed the geographic feature Cape Kennedy. The locals were never happy with the renaming, and so in 1973 the Florida State Legislature passed a law restoring the 400-year-old name. The Kennedy Space Center retains its name.

Cape Canaveral has been a rocket launch site since 1950. The cape was chosen because rockets fired east gain momentum from the east-moving rotation of the Earth, and the closer to the equator the bigger the gain. It was also chosen because the immediate downrange trajectory is the ocean expanse of the Atlantic. Jules Verne chose Florida as the launch site in his 1865 novel *From the Earth to the Moon*, although his site was twenty miles east of Tampa, not Cape Canaveral.

The Redstone and Atlas rockets used for Mercury, and the Titan II used for Gemini, were all far smaller than the Saturn V, and far less complicated. The Saturn V was three and a half times taller than the Titan II, almost five times taller than either the Mercury Redstone or the Atlas, with a diameter far larger than any of the other three. The smaller rockets were prepped at the actual launch site.

The Redstone, assembled horizontally in a hangar, required not much prep. It could be lifted whole and horizontally by crane at the launch site. The Atlas was an ICBM that could be stored horizontally, transported horizontally, then pivoted upright onto the launching pad. The Titan II was trucked in sections to the launch pad and then assembled, requiring a more involved and longer prep time.

On-site preparation was not possible for the Saturn V. Months of preparation could not take place in an exposed setting in salt air. As just one example, the three Saturn V stages were made by different contractors. When they were mated was the first time one stage touched the one above, or the one below. For the second stage both the one above and the one below, and for the third stage the instrument unit above, the brain of the Saturn V. The Saturn V was a remarkable collection of systems and subsystems, and so the rocket as a whole used the instrument unit to communicate with itself. When one stage was mated to another all the connections – mechanical, electrical, and fluid – had to be confirmed so the instrument unit could do its job. This could not happen in rain driven by a forty-mile-per-hour wind.

And so the Vehicle Assembly Building (VAB) was conceived.

Urbahn Architects began designing the VAB in 1962, with construction beginning in 1963. Reflected in the design was the optimism and expectations found in the early Apollo years when the inventors of Apollo envisioned dozens of Saturn V launches per year. The building has four bays. Three were outfitted for Apollo and the Saturn V, with the forth held in reserve for a more powerful version of the Saturn V, which would have required work platforms at levels different from the Apollo Saturn V.

The VAB was designed to be expandable into six bays, and the roof was designed to be heightened to accommodate a Mars rocket, which would have been much taller than the Saturn V, requiring more space above for the cranes that assembled the stages. Even today vertical girders can be seen protruding through the roof as an expired anticipation, a de facto monument to what was once imagined, once intended.

As Apollo was scaled back there would never be a reason to raise the roof, or to expand the VAB to six bays. The three bays dedicated to Apollo were never all in use at the same time.

When the VAB was completed in 1966, it was the largest building in the world by volume. Even with its eight-acre footprint, the 528-foot-tall building (almost a cube) defies gaining a sense of its proportion. Because the VAB is on flat land with the Atlantic behind, and because the only nearby structures are launch towers, reckoning its size is difficult, if not impossible for the lay observer.

Each bay has a segmented vertical door that opens to a height of 454 feet. The entire height of the Statue of Liberty and its pedestal could fit easily in any bay. That's how big the VAB is. In a very real sense the VAB, an extraordinary work of architecture and of civil engineering, is, once again, just the sort of cathedral America builds. As David West Reynolds expressed so eloquently in his book *Kennedy Space Center – Gateway to Space*, "The entire creation and assembly process culminated in the heart of the VAB. VAB technicians, from crane operators to engineers, felt the importance of their work deeply and could not have been more committed or dedicated if they had been installing the stained glass window in Notre Dame Cathedral, a task that might have been undertaken by their forebearers. The magnitude of the effort was comparable. Both monuments expressed the power of shared faith in something beyond the ordinary, in a purpose beyond simple explanation. In both cases, the height of the achievement would reach beyond simple measure."

The Mobile Launch Platform

A Saturn V with preparation complete contained an implicit question. How does this behemoth get from the VAB to the launch pad? The Saturn V was thirty-six stories tall, but the VAB is fifty-two stories. Sure, the cranes need overhead room to operate, but another sixteen stories?

Yep.

Early on in the development of the Saturn V came the realization that the months needed for the huge rocket's assembly and preparation for launch would need to happen inside. Hence the VAB. But, still, how to transport a Saturn V to the launch pad?

At first, Kurt Debus, overall director of launch operations, and Roco Petrone, director of Saturn V launches, made a casual assumption – that barges would be used to transport the Saturn V. Across history barges in rivers and canals had carried very heavy loads. Soon enough, however, the idea became not only prohibitively expensive, but unworkable.

Debus and Petrone had already enlisted Don Buchanan, an engineer's engineer, to study the barge concept. First a canal would need to be dug, of course. But it would cut across three-and-a half-miles of the facility, requiring numerous draw bridges. And then, Buchanan realized, wind would hit the rocket and the tower as if they were sails, requiring constant maneuvering of the barge to keep it in the middle of the canal. Plus, the backwash from the number of powerful engines needed would have caused swirling havoc reflected off the walls of the canal in waters that needed to be pretty much calm. Imagine the Washington Monument rocking to-and-fro, and then falling over.

When Buchanan had finished tallying the drawbacks of a canal-and-barge system time was tight. Debus needed to know: if not a barge, then what? Once again, that Apollo serendipity emerged. If not a barge then what? The answer would be found in the coal fields of western Kentucky.

By chance, or serendipity, a man named Barry Schlenk was in Huntsville a few days after Debus's call for an answer. Schlenk was there to discuss overhead cranes for the assembly of Titan rockets. And once again by chance, he overheard a conversation about the problem of transporting the Saturn V. Maybe, Schlenk wondered, these NASA folks would like to hear about the machine his company produced. A giant machine that stripped off soil to expose coal seams.

The initial response from Debus was a no, but then, heck, why not go to Kentucky to see this machine and report back why the idea won't work. Buchanan, along with three representatives from Debus's office, did so. What they observed was the giant machine, with tank treads on each corner. They further observed that it could carry a tremendous load without vibrating, and that it was self-leveling. By failing in their mission to gain evidence as to why the idea wouldn't work these men succeeded in moving the Saturn V.

The Mobile Launch Platform – the crawler – would be much larger than the strip mining colossus Buchanan observed, but the basic concept and design held – a platform with tank treads on each corner. The platform measured 131 feet by 114 feet, or about one third of an acre. A typical lot for a suburban house then was about one quarter of an acre. In the middle of the platform was a square hole forty-five feet on each side to allow the rocket exhaust to continue downward and be directed by the concrete flame diverter built into the soil below the parked platform.

The crawler was built by the Marion Power Shovel Company of Marion, Ohio, which had provided steam shovels for constructing the Panama Canal.

Curiously, the crawler was not a new idea. In the early 1950s von Braun envisioned a very similar mobile platform. That the idea was lost and rediscovered seems highly unlikely. True, many of von Braun's post-war spaceflight ideas and concepts were beyond the technologies, materials, and practical know-how of the day. His assumptions regarding problem solving were sometimes optimistic to the point of approaching science fiction. As such, Buchanan might have concluded this monstrous machine was impossible – especially one self-leveling and free of vibration – until he saw it wasn't.

Not only was the crawler platform a feat exemplar of mechanical engineering, so was the actual mobile launch tower atop the platform, built by Ingalls Iron Works of Pascagoula, Mississippi.

The purpose of the launch tower was to provide work platforms at specific levels along the length of the rocket, and to provide electrical connections, plus propellant and pneumatic lines, at various points for each stage. Although a Saturn V left the VAB prepped, except for fueling, that preparation had to be maintained by these connections.

The tower held two high-speed elevators to reach the work platforms. An overhead crane topped out the tower. The most notable features, however, were the nine swing arms containing the connection points, as well as the four hold-down arms. These four arms held the rocket erect and in place during transport, and then during launch they prevented the rocket from rising until thrust had reached launch specifications.

The swing arms were Alabama creations, difficult projects for the Brown Engineering Company of Huntsville, and for the Hayes International Corporation of Birmingham, the fabricator. Construction of the swing arms began while the Saturn V was in mid development, leading to frequently changing specifications for the arms. In addition, the arms were unique, unprecedented designs of extraordinary complexity. Weighing an average of twenty-two tons, each ten-foot-wide arm carried dozens of electrical and fluid connections. When the time came for the verb in their name to activate, the arms had to swing away from the rocket in nine seconds.

Without much surprise, then, the projected cost of the swing arms, $11.5 million, tripled, given the changing specifications and the expected setbacks when designing and building such complex devices. Despite these problems, which were often ongoing, the swing arms worked flawlessly. In fact, magnificently.

This is why the VAB was designed to be fifty-two stories – 525 feet. The Saturn V with the escape tower was 375 feet as placed on the deck of the crawler, allowing for the eighteen-feet-tall F1 engine nozzles that were below the deck, in the square hole. The deck of the crawler was already twenty-five feet above the floor of the VAB, so the top of the assembled rocket was 400 feet, plus the top of the 398-foot umbilical tower was at 423 feet, leaving just over 100 feet of headroom for the huge cranes to be anchored, and to maneuver.

Both the Vehicle Assembly Building and the Mobile Launch Platform remain remarkable pieces of design, engineering, and fabrication, two facets of the overall Apollo program often eclipsed by the prominence and magnificence of the Saturn V.

6

Let's begin evaluating just what the Apollo Application Program could have been, might have been.

The early astronauts were known by name and face to just about any American who picked up a paper or watched the evening news. Across media – print and electronic – the original Mercury Seven were promoted not only for newsworthiness, but also by specific calculation by NASA and various media journalists.[11] The journalists, in the early years, pursued and cultivated a relationship with NASA, of course. Soon after NASA would cultivate a relationship with journalists.

No venue promoted the astronauts more than *Life* magazine. Across media outlets, the ink and words and images were virtually all positive, but *Life,* in particular, portrayed these seven Americans very often as overgrown Boy Scouts. Godless commies rule? Not on your life, pal!

Life was a hugely successful weekly magazine that typically featured images over words, although certainly not always. The editors understood early on that the Mercury Seven, and their families, would be media gold. As government employees, information about the astronauts was in the public domain, but NASA, in a controversial move, approved a contract giving *Life* exclusive rights to the individual stories of the astronauts. The astronauts were provided life insurance policies by the magazine, and were paid for their stories, supplementing their government salaries, although the salaries were well above the national average. In 1961 the average family income was about

$5,700. The original astronauts were paid from about $8,300 to $12,500, depending on experience.

These personal histories were ghost written and typically cleaned up. There was truth to this apple pie portrayal, however varying. John Glenn fit that tan and green badge-laden uniform image the best. Some of the others, not so much. After all, they were recruited from the test pilot cadre. You know, those with the Right Stuff.

Some of those stuffed with that Right Stuff who remained high flying and incredibly fast flying stick-and-rudder men mocked these seven, calling them "spam in a can." But no matter. These seven were now all but going to save America, and get us ahead of those pesky Russians.

Such notoriety, to the point of heroic fame and celebrity, dropped off significantly with the next groups of astronauts.[12] The fame and celebrity reemerged predictably with Apollo 11, with Armstrong and Aldrin and Collins, then dropped away again in the eyes of John and Jane Doe.

And so in this respect, NASA was something like Hollywood. We know the faces on the wide screen because, well, they're on the screen. But what about the other side of the camera, the many other sides? The cinematographers, the directors, the sound crews? The screenwriters? The lighting techs, the set designers, the costumers? The film developers, the editors, the foley artists, the special effects artists? Those working at Panavision? The distributors and the local theater owners? Hundreds of people are involved directly in one major film production, into the thousands for a blockbuster, and there are hundreds more involved indirectly.

BEYOND 17: THE APOLLO APPLICATIONS PROGRAM AND LOSING THE NEW FRONTIER

Landing men on the moon, likewise, employed thousands of workers virtually unsung beyond the astronauts themselves. Engineers, physicists, chemists, geologists, astronomers, meteorologists. Skilled managers. Machinists. Computer whizzes as they existed then. And so on. And so on even more. By the thousands. By the tens of thousands, really. Actually, by the hundreds of thousands. All told, 400,000 people worked to get Apollo off the ground that is Earth and onto the regolith of the lunar surface. And back. In one piece.

Imagine that. Figuring out just how to send human beings to another heavenly body. To go from the surface of the blue and green and wet place we call home to land of "magnificent desolation," as Buzz Aldrin described his lunar prospect. How utterly and wholly remarkable.

Homo sapiens have been around about 300,000 years. Countless many across the millennia did imagine. And then, 299,950 or so years later, 400,000 homo sapiens not only imagined such a trek, they wrought the essence of it and dragged it into reality.

The Apollo Applications Program was a nod to many of those 400,000 and their jobs.

***

What would eventually become the Apollo Applications Program (AAP) began in early 1964 when President Johnson directed NASA to specify plans for human spaceflight beyond the initial Apollo landings. Apollo's price tag would total more than $25 billion and Johnson figured to not overlook any dividend from the investment.

Initially known as the Apollo Extension Systems (AES), then Saturn-Apollo Applications (SAA), by 1967 the project had become known as AAP, the nomenclature change happening somewhat informally.

The first projects were to be underway even before the first lunar landing. These initial projects would have been Earth-orbit missions, including the first small space station; gaining experience in extravehicular activity (maneuvering and working in space itself); and a manned orbiting telescope. Further projects would have included missions in lunar orbit, and extended lunar surface missions.

Besides creating and continuing an expanding presence on the moon, a key goal of AAP was continuity of experience and basic research, including applications to rocket technology, and of the technologies to maintain human life. Also, to conduct scientific research in alien settings, to develop the logistics of space flight, and to develop methods of locomotion on alien worlds. All with an eye on a mid-1980s mission to Mars.

Referring to the *Apollo Application Program Summary Report* released by NASA in February 1969, the broad goals of the program were:

- Use of launch vehicles and spacecraft developed for Apollo

- Re-visit, re-supply, re-use, repair
- Open-ended mission philosophy
- Maximum utilization of existing hardware
- Develop techniques and expand basis of knowledge

More specifically, from the same report and regarding the first phase of AAP:

- Long duration space flights of men and systems. 1) Unique capabilities of man, 2) Habitability, 3) Biomedical/behavioral, 4) Systems development

- Scientific investigations in Earth orbit. 1) Solar astronomy, 2) Earth observations, 3) Stellar astronomy

- Applications in Earth orbit. 1) Meteorology, 2) Earth resources, 3) Communications

- Effective and economical approach to the development of a basis for potential future space programs.

AAP is now referred to in the past conditional tense because of the Congress at the time. In 1964, the Future Programs Task Group was given the job, as per Johnson's request, of defining NASA's goals beyond the early lunar landings. The Group submitted a report to James Webb in early 1965, outlining the use of existing Apollo technology and hardware to pursue this direction.

As noted NASA's budget peaked in 1966 at $5.93 billion, or 4.4% of the Federal budget. After this peak, NASA's budget declined in roughly a straight line, to $4.97 billion in 1967, eventually reaching $3.75 billion in 1970, or less than 2% of the Federal budget. During this decline AAP was particularly hard hit. The Johnson administration's 1967 funding request for AAP was $270 million, but just $80 million was allocated. Ironically, by 1967 the annual cost of fighting in Vietnam was approaching a peak.

A few AAP projects would be completed, but AAP was gutted from the start. The hoped-for continuity of space technology and experience never got off the ground. Literally.

Referring to the list of names from Chapter 1 who were instrumental in bringing about 7-20-69, Lyndon Johnson's name also belongs on that list. As vice president, Johnson was chairman of the National Aeronautics and Space Council, making key decisions about early U.S. manned spaceflight and about Apollo.

However, including Johnson's name comes with a bit of irony. Although Johnson remained a solid supporter of Apollo and the space program personally, his administration was focused on the social programs of his Great Society initiative. Johnson wanted to remain within the overall federal budget for each year as he implemented these social programs. Among many others, the programs included Medicare, Medicaid, Head Start, the National Endowment for the Arts, the National Endowment for the Humanities, Public Broadcasting Service, and National Public Radio. The continuing expenditures in Vietnam also sapped the federal budget in those years, and beyond. Despite the president's enthusiasm for space exploration, including manned space exploration, applications of Apollo technology and experience were not at the top of the Johnson administration's list. In Congress, Apollo applications were pretty much not anywhere on any list.

On March 31, 1968, Johnson informed the nation he would not seek re-election the following November. Republican Richard Nixon would win the 1968 election. In his inaugural address he said, "Let us go to the new worlds together – not as new worlds to be conquered, but as a new adventure to be shared." These words were mostly political theater, darkening any remaining hopes of an active and ongoing AAP.

7

As noted, AAP emerged out of the earlier AES and SAA. In 1964, James Webb, in response to President Johnson's request for a long-range manned spaceflight plan from NASA, formed an inhouse Future Programs Task Group. In early 1965, the group delivered its report to Webb. This earlier group recommended a future program based on existing Apollo hardware, an idea AAP would continue to a lesser degree. Specifically, the hardware being the CSM, the LM, the Saturn 1B, and the Saturn V. SAA was planned at two possible levels. The first level was somewhat more ambitious than AAP. The second level was far more ambitious than AAP.

From the point of view of NASA planners in 1965 the first lunar landing would happen no later than early 1968. These planners expected production of CSMs, LMs, and Saturn 1B and Saturn V rockets to continue over the next four years *by the dozens.*

The more ambitious SAA plan assumed twenty-six Saturn 1B and seventeen Saturn V launches between 1968 and 1975. The majority of missions would have been in Earth orbit, gaining experience in human physiology on long duration flights, as well as experience in assembling spacecraft modules in orbit. Many of these missions included scientific experiments, including astronomical instruments for observing across the electromagnetic spectrum. Three SAA missions in 1970 were scheduled to be the next lunar landings after the completion of the initial landings.

In response to slashed NASA budgets, by 1966 SAA had become AAP. The expectations of producing Apollo components, Saturn 1Bs, and Saturn Vs by the dozens were relegated to a dreamworld. Despite President Johnson's advocacy for SAA and then AAP, Congress did not provide viable funding, in large measure due to the cost of supporting the war in Vietnam.

Then the Apollo 1 fire in January of 1967. By that time many members of Congress had already questioned not only the cost of Apollo, but also the very purpose of the program. Congress used the tragedy to take NASA to task, focusing on Apollo, providing only $122 million for AAP. Johnson had requested $455 million. Not only had AAP emerged initially as a pared down SAA, the program itself would be further pared.

From NASA's point of view in 1966, the first AAP missions would take place before the first lunar landing, and then alternate with the landing missions, thereby having Apollo continuity well in place as the initial landings concluded.

Again referencing the *Apollo Applications Program Summary Report* from February 1969 the initial mission concepts were use of launch vehicles and spacecraft for Apollo; re-visit, re-supply, re-use, repair; open-ended mission philosophy; maximum utilization of existing hardware; developing operating techniques and expand basis of knowledge.

The AAP was divided into three areas:

- Earth orbit, with altitudes varying from Low Earth orbit (LEO) to synchronous orbit at an altitude of 22,300 miles

- Lunar orbit, primarily to map the complete lunar surface

- Lunar surface

The AAP timeline was divided into four sections:

- Phase 1, 1969-1971. Phase 1 included the initial lunar missions, gaining experience in landing on the moon, exploring the lunar surface, and living on the moon. Apollo 11 to Apollo 14 corresponded approximately to Phase 1. As well, Phase 1 included a small space station in Earth orbit.

- Phase 2, 1972-1973. Phase 2 would begin lunar exploration. The missions would be equipped for longer stays and would include the lunar rover as part of the payload.

Apollo 15 to Apollo 17 corresponded approximately to Phase 2.

- Phase 3, 1974. Phase 3 would see two astronauts in the CSM in a polar lunar orbit for twenty-eight days of reconnaissance.

- Phase 4, 1975-1976. Phase 4 would begin extended lunar stays, initially up to fourteen days. Missions would include dual launches. The first launch would deliver a modified lunar payload module (LPM), which was an LM with the ascent stage removed, along with that stage's fuel tanks and other equipment removed, providing cubic footage for food, water, oxygen, and scientific equipment. The LPM would remain quiescent for up to three months. The second launch would land the astronauts near the awaiting shelter. This initial foray would eventually lead to larger shelters and an expanding lunar base for six men to spend up to six months on the moon.

Earth-Orbital Missions

The first AAP missions were to be in Earth orbit. The primary mission was an orbiting station called a "wet workshop," so named because a Saturn S-IVB stage (the third stage of a Saturn V, the second stage of a Saturn 1B) would have been placed in orbit after firing. The "wet" description acknowledged that fuel had been in the tank. Any residual fuel would have been purged.

A hatch designed into the top of the hydrogen tank would have allowed for the insertion of the cylinder containing lab equipment, living quarters, and life support. This cylinder would have been on the top of the rocket stack, in place of the LM. At the top of the fuel tank would be placed a multiple docking adapter (MDA), a pressurized segment that would have allowed the CSM, the Apollo Telescope Mount (ATM) for solar observation, and an optical telescope to all dock simultaneously.

Medical observers were part of the crew for the purpose of collecting data on the effects of long-term weightlessness. Extended EVAs were planned to gain experience in zero-g tool use and repair/maintenance techniques.

The basic idea turned into the "dry workshop" of Skylab. The "dry" description refers to Skylab being a lab purpose-built on Earth then launched ready to use into orbit.

Also suggested was the Apollo Manned Survey mission. This mission would have been conducted from an altered and repurposed CSM. Geological, agricultural, oceanographic, and other data about Earth would be gathered.

BEYOND 17: THE APOLLO APPLICATIONS PROGRAM AND LOSING THE NEW FRONTIER

Lunar-Orbital Mission

Using an array of instruments, including a magnetometer, a radar altimeter gamma-ray spectrometer, a micrometeorite collection plate, and standard film cameras the crew would observe the whole of the lunar surface. The project was cancelled when the Lunar Orbiter, an unmanned moon satellite using classified photography and transmission technology, provided all the survey information needed.

Lunar Surface Missions

The following components comprised the initial lunar base concept within AES. A lunar base would have been the most ambitious undertaking of AAP.

In the broadest definition, the initial lunar landings were considered the first phase of a lunar base, which in fact each was, particularly Apollo 15, 16, and 17. Compared to less than one day for Apollo 11, these later missions spent about three days on the moon, and so the CSM spent more time in lunar orbit. These initial landings held the purpose of delivering enough basic experience of landing on the moon and launching, traversing the regolith, craters, hills, and escarpments of the lunar surface, and living there – surviving there, at this point – briefly. Apollo 18, 19, and 20 would have continued this initial buildup of experience.

Modified LMs were key to phase 2, establishing a basic lunar base. The LM contained separate descent and ascent engines. When astronauts launched from the moon to return to the CSM in lunar orbit only the cabin part of the overall lander launched. Left behind was the bottom section, comprised of the landing legs and the descent engine. Engineers realized that a LM without an ascent engine and with those fuel tanks removed created significant additional cubic footage for supplies, and a third astronaut. Removing the ascent engine meant, of course, that the entire modified LM, including the cabin, would land on the moon and then remain permanently.

The modified LMs would serve four functions: ATM, LM taxi, LM truck, LM shelter.

The ATM was designed as a solar telescope. The original ATM design was a deployable unit essentially replacing the Advanced Orbiting Solar Observatory, cancelled in 1965. It was attached to the service module. The service module was the single-engine rocket attached to the command module. Together the two components were the CSM.

This idea evolved quickly into housing the ATM in a modified LM. Once in orbit, the ATM with a three-man crew would dock with a CSM or a Saturn S-IVB orbiting workshop. The crew would conduct the observations and experiments, returning to Earth in the command module, leaving the ATM in orbit for the next crew. As funding for AAP continued to fall, the modified LM approach was dropped and the ATM became a non-independent part of Skylab.

The ATM carried eight major observational instruments, plus a number of second tier instruments. The ATM made observations along the x-ray, ultraviolet, and visible light spectrums, as well as other spectrums. The ATM was one of the most successful facets of Skylab. (See chapter 9). Over the three missions more than 150,000 exposures were made of the sun.

The ATM also saved Skylab. During the launch of Skylab one of two solar panels was ripped away. The second jammed and could not be deployed fully. The electrical supply to Skylab was reduced severely. The ATM had its own windmill-shaped solar array, which was undamaged. An in-orbit rewiring scheme allowed the ATM solar panels to power Skylab.

The LM taxi was the standard LM, with all capabilities. It was beefed up with additional oxygen, water, LH2 and lox tanks (liquid hydrogen and liquid oxygen), and heavier micrometeorite and radiation shielding. Additionally, space was provided for a third astronaut, the command module pilot. Once landed the crew would transfer to the already-landed LM shelter to begin expeditions lasting from two weeks to three months. Unlike the other modified LM versions, the LM taxi retained its ascent engine. However, once the crew transferred from the LM taxi to the CSM, that particular LM taxi was obsolete, having used both its descent and ascent engines. Like the ascent stages of Apollo missions 11, 12, 14, 15, 16, and 17, an LM taxi ascent stage would orbit briefly before crashing into the regolith.

The LM truck was built on an LM descent stage. The cargo platform, utilizing the space of the ascent engine, could hold 11,000 pounds of equipment and supplies for delivery to the lunar surface. Unmanned, the LM truck would be landed from the CSM by remote control. The LM truck could also land without human help by utilizing radio beacons already in place on the moon. The LM truck would be waiting for the next lunar landing crew.

The LM shelter would be landed remotely to await from weeks to months for a crew to arrive. Without the ascent engine and without fuel tanks for that engine, cubic footage became available for scientific equipment and consumables for human life, initially allowing a fourteen-day stay for a crew of two. A lunar rover was also stowed in the LM shelter. Reflecting the expected continuing supply of Saturn Vs an LM shelter mission required two Saturn V launches. The first launch, with a three-man crew in the CSM, would land the LM shelter on the moon remotely. After an orbital surveying mission, the crew would return to Earth. A second Saturn V would launch weeks to months later with the crew to occupy the shelter.

In those later missions the full crew of the CSM would take an LM taxi to the surface, leaving the CSM in orbit and unmanned. The astronauts would then begin a thirty-day stay.

Both the LM truck and the LM shelter, their ascent engines removed, would stay on the moon permanently.

Phase 4 would have concluded the initial Apollo Applications Program.

8

The idea of a lunar base predates Alan Shepard's first flight. The original U.S. vision of a lunar base dates from 1958. The Lunex proposal came from an Air Force study that envisioned a twenty-one-man underground base on the moon by 1968. The project would have utilized a rocket system significantly different from the Saturn family, including solid fuel boosters.

The Horizon Lunar Outpost was a 1959 proposal from the U.S. Army for a military outpost on the moon. The goal was a twelve-man permanent outpost by 1966. Reflecting the optimism of the time, both within the larger culture and the military industrial complex, establishing the base would have required hundreds of Saturn I and Saturn II launches, more than five per month during the initial buildup.

Project Selena was a 1964 U.S. proposal by aeronautical engineer Philip Bono. His idea was one of remarkable vision and scope.

Project Selena was based on an envisioned huge rocket called ROMBUS (**R**eusable **O**rbit-**M**odule **B**ooster and **U**tility **S**huttle). ROMBUS was a single-stage-to-orbit craft that would fly to the moon from LEO, land, launch, and return to LEO. After landing on the moon the rocket's liquid hydrogen (LH2) tanks, now empty, would be left behind to be retrofitted into habitation modules. Early missions would leave behind two LH2 tanks, later missions four.

Bono envisioned a lunar base of 1,000 by 1984, built up over an eight-year period. The base development would have required over 1300 ROMBUS launches. A key purpose of the base would have been to launch unmanned cargo missions to Mars to support a 1986 manned Mars mission.

From our point of view today, the numbers and concepts in the previous paragraphs seem ridiculous. Although Bono's ideas often competed successfully on design and cost with more traditional approaches, they received little recognition, and were in fact risky. Still, Bono's ideas convey the fertile creativity and optimism of the time.

From 1962 to 1974, the Soviets studied three separate lunar base ideas. All were based on utilizing the ill-fated N1 rocket. Ironically, despite no human having ventured beyond Earth orbit since 1972, and despite a need for a new generation of heavy-lift rockets, the lunar base concept continued. A 1988 Soviet study was based on utilizing the successful Energia booster.

From 1989 to 1997, at least seven U.S. lunar base studies were undertaken. Outpost to the Moon, 1987; Lunar Evolution Base, 1989; Lunar Outpost, 1989; First Lunar Outpost, 1992; Lunox (not Lunex), 1993; Human Lunar Return, 1996; LANTR (LOX-Augmented Nuclear Thermal Rocket) Moon Base, 1997. Although surely pursued seriously by those making the proposals and designing the bases, we can only assume that at higher levels such studies were mostly PR pieces, or at best the expression of gossamer hopes. At no time did funding for these projects exist.

Lunar base ideas continue today. In 2007, China began its lunar exploration program with a series of Chang'e missions, 1-5. Chang'e 1 was launched October 27, a surveying lunar orbiter, as was Chang'e 2, launched October 1, 2010. Chang'e 3, launched December 1, 2013, soft landed on the moon with a rover. Chang'e 4, launched December 7, 2018, was the first spacecraft to soft land on the far side of the moon. Chang'e 5, launched November 23, 2020, returned to Earth about three weeks later with lunar samples.

In June of 2021, China and Russia announced the two nations would cooperate in building a lunar base, inviting international cooperation. Interest has been scant. The schedule states a completion date of 2035, although that date should be seen as very preliminary. Russia is quite the junior partner, and the technological advancements needed, while in theory possible, are vastly optimistic.

***

A U.S. lunar base would have grown from evolving projects. AES first, leading to the Apollo Logistics Support System (ALSS), and then the Lunar Exploration System for Apollo in two stages (LESA I and LESA II). In order for the next phase to utilize and build on existing hardware, the projects were not defined precisely, and so were somewhat fluid from one to the next. From a 1966 point of view the phases would have proceeded thusly:

- Two men on the lunar surface for 2 days. Apollo 14 accomplished this.

- Two men on the lunar surface for 14 to 30 days (AES) utilizing the LM shelter

- Two men on the lunar surface for 14 to 30 days using a STEP shelter (an expanded LM shelter) or a MOLAB (see below in ALSS)

- Three men on the lunar surface for 90 days (LESA I)

- Three men on the lunar surface for 90 days with a MOLAB (see ALSS) (LESA I)

- Six men on the lunar surface for 180 days with an expanded shelter and an extended range MOLAB-type rover (LESA II)

Although ALSS and LESA were costly – $500 million for ALSS, $1.5 billion for LESA – both projects would have been far more efficient than the actual Apollo landings in terms of the number of men on the lunar surface, the number of exploration days, the lunar area explored, and the number of Saturn V launches needed.

Interestingly, because of the much smaller size of the moon compared to Earth, line-of-sight radio communication would be greatly reduced. Without a triad of communications satellites in lunar orbit radio signals from one lunar location intended for more distant lunar locations would be relayed from the main lunar base to Earth stations, then transmitted back to rovers and outposts on the moon.

ALSS

ALSS was dependent on the LM truck. Again, the LM truck was the descent stage of the original LM with a cargo platform in place of the ascent stage. The LM truck would have been used to land the LM shelter (chapter 7), or the MOLAB. The MOLAB, a pressurized **MO**bile **LAB**oratory, was intended for fourteen-day expeditions by a two-man crew with an ability to cover hundreds of miles.

In addition to the LM truck and the LM taxi, ALSS would have required the continuing production of Saturn Vs (recall the projected six bays in the VAB); an expanded CSM, capable of transporting up to four astronauts to lunar orbit; and a lunar flying vehicle, with which a MOLAB crew could return to base in case of breakdown. On Apollo 15, 16, and 17 crews could not drive the lunar roving vehicle (LRV) farther than walking distance back to the LM. This regulation was based on the consumables in their life support backpacks more than the astronauts' stamina.

MOLAB and the lunar flying vehicles were under the general heading of MOBEV, Lunar Surface **MOB**ility Systems and **EV**olution. The lunar flyers included were the MOBEV F1B, MOBEV F2E, and MOBEV F2B. The F1B and F2B were for surface-to-surface transportation. The F1B was basically a flying pogo stick, while the F2B and the F2E were flying benches, both holding two astronauts. The F2E was capable of achieving orbit and emergency rendezvous with the CSM.

Other designs under MOBEV included LRV designs form various companies, mobile laboratory designs other than MOLAB, and the R1CB, a combination backhoe and dump truck.

LESA

LESA was similar in design to the LM, but much larger. A LESA craft would have landed on four legs under its own power, delivered to lunar orbit by a Saturn V.

LESA would have used a new lunar landing vehicle with the same basic configuration of the LM, but much larger, the Lunar Adapter Surface Station (LASS).

LASS as an acronym first meant Lunar Applications of a spent S-IVB/IU Stage. IU was for instrument unit, the brains of the Saturn V, located between the top of the third stage and the LM, which was below the CSM. This initial meaning concerned the wet workshop orbiting lab concept, which was later replaced by Skylab.

The second meaning, within the LESA concept, concerned a long-term shelter. Although similar to the LM shelter, the LASS was larger and carried consumables for a two-man crew to stay ninety-six days. The LASS also carried 4,000 pounds of scientific equipment, a LRV, a LFU, and 5,000 pounds of fuel for those vehicles. (The LRV and LFU will be covered in a following section.) The LASS was a turnkey mini lunar base, whereas the LM shelter was in fact a repurposed LM – perhaps similar to comparing a camper top in a pickup bed to a small RV.

Curiously, the LASS was launched already docked with the CSM; i.e., reversed with its rocket pointed up, with a protective faring above the Apollo capsule for aerodynamic effect. The CSM rocket braked the LASS to place it in lunar orbit, then undocked. A LM descent engine then landed the LASS on the lunar surface. Later the two-man crew would arrive by LM taxi in a second launch. The CSM commander would then return to Earth alone, rather than spend almost 100 days by himself orbiting the moon. Three months later a CSM would return with a lone astronaut to rendezvous with the LM taxi.

This new lander would have a descent stage only, with the LESA shelter above. It was designed for a crew of six, with three astronauts inhabiting the shelter at first. Initial missions would be ninety days, later missions 180 days.

Above the descent stage was an interior domed cylinder, housing the living quarters of about 1000 cubic meters. This space was surrounded by an outer workspace ring. Both areas were tall enough to stand in and spacious enough to walk about. The workspace ring could accommodate astronauts in pressure suits in the event of emergency depressurization.

Above the living and work areas was stowed the MOLAB. Although the LM taxi would have been employed with LESA, the LM truck would not have been needed. The MOLAB delivered by LM truck under ALSS, or delivered in the LASS landing craft had LESA moved forward, illustrates the fluidity between the three basic concepts.

Of the many designs put forward in the first part of the 1960s to travel the moon, both on the surface and above the surface, only the LRV was built, used on Apollo missions 15, 16, and 17.

The idea of exploring the lunar surface faster than the human gait in a pressure suit had been around since the *Collier's* magazine exposé from the early 1950s. Those earlier ideas were closer to fantasy than a possible reality.

In the 1960s, elaborate designs emerged, often with pressurized cabins, such as the MOLAB. Many designs were based on the assumption of a continuing supply of Saturn Vs. In those early days a typical lunar mission was seen as a dual-launch project, using one Saturn V to deliver equipment, including rovers, and a second to deliver the crew. As the scope of Apollo was reduced in the mid-1960s such elaborate vehicles remained on drafting tables. With Apollo missions now being single-launch projects any lunar rover would need to be stowed in the LM.

The vehicle built, the LRV, had no pressurized cabin, or any cabin. The LRV found the limits of basic lunar transportation – it was pretty much two lawn chairs on a platform with electrically-powered wheels on each corner. To call the LRV an overgrown go kart is not so inaccurate. It weighed just 460 pounds on Earth.

Studies for workable LRVs had been ongoing throughout the 1960s. Von Braun established a Lunar Rover Task Team at Marshall Spaceflight Center. However, not until just days before Armstrong and Aldrin landed did Marshall present a proposal for final development of the LRV. Boeing, Bendix, Grumman, and Chrysler were interested. Boeing was awarded the contract in October of 1969, and would work closely with the Defense Research Laboratories of General Motors. Essentially GM supplied the vehicle and Boeing supplied the electronics and the navigation system.

Once again the Apollo serendipity was in play. Although some problems emerged in production, of course, just seventeen months passed from the awarding of the contract to Boeing to the delivery of the first LRV on April 1, 1971. That first LRV was launched on Apollo 15, July 26, 1971. All three LRVs performed virtually flawlessly.

AES, SAA, and AAP did not have clear demarcations along a timeline. Although AAP was formally started in 1965, the program was an inclusion of the previous programs, which continued informally beyond 1965 in terms of their objectives. By 1969, however, AAP was a standalone program with the earlier nomenclatures now part of its history. ALSS and LESA, as envisioned under the earlier programs, were now, to whatever extent they might be realized, informally under AAP.

The inclusion, though, was not a sum equal to the various parts of AES and SAA, or of ALSS and LESA concepts. With reduced funding AAP was now a whole less than the sum of its constituent parts.

9

The Apollo Applications Program was not a complete washout. However, the missions that did fly in the mid-1970s, after Apollo 17, might be described almost as leftovers. At any rate, this smattering of missions did not provide the continuity of spaceflight technology and of spaceflight experience the original vision of AAP would have pursued, a continuity that, from a 1966 viewpoint, would likely include a Mars mission in the mid-1980s.

The missions were Skylab (with the Apollo Telescope Mount), Apollo-Soyuz, and Voyager.

SKYLAB

Skylab remains the only space station to be operated by the U.S. exclusively. Space Station Freedom was proposed by President Ronald Reagan in 1984. Frequent demands from Congress for redesigns, as well as balking about the cost, kept pushing Freedom further into the future. By 1993 the project was a political no go.

In that same year the idea of space station Freedom transformed into the International Space Station (ISS). Funding for Freedom was shifted to the U. S.'s share of ISS. In addition to NASA, the other space agencies involved in the development and cost of ISS were Roscosmos (Russia), JAXA (Japan), ESA (European coalition), and CSA (Canada).

AAP envisioned a basic space station built in and from the spent S-II second stage of a Saturn V. This plan would have required purging any existing hydrogen fuel, and then inserting the lab and living quarters as a module into the stage through a large hatch. Skylab, though, would be built as a dedicated lab and living quarters from the start, using S-IVB stages.

In the original AAP plans the ATM would have been an independently operating telescope in a converted LM. It was later incorporated integrally into Skylab. Solar observation and data collection advanced significantly using the telescope.

Skylab was in orbit from May 1973 to February 1974. The space station hosted three crews of three astronauts each, known as Skylab missions 2, 3, and 4. (Mission 1 was the initial placing into orbit.) Still, during that time dozens of experiments were carried out, including experiments in life sciences, solar physics and astronomy, Earth resources, and material science. In addition, nineteen student-submitted experiments were on Skylab missions.

Although preliminary plans were for the Space Shuttle to re-boost Skylab into a stable orbit, the Shuttle was not ready in time. Due in part to increased solar activity increasing atmospheric drag on the station, Skylab's orbit decayed and on July 11, 1979 the station entered the atmosphere. As the station broke up some parts burned during reentry. Other parts impacted the Indian Ocean and an area in Western Australia.

McDonnel Douglas built two Skylab modules. The second, to be named Skylab B, was planned for launch in 1975 or 1976. Part of Skylab B's purpose was in conjunction with the Apollo-Soyuz mission, and to possibly combine with the Soviet Salyut station. Later to be known as Advanced Skylab, the module would have been used, and expanded, in conjunction with the Shuttle.

Skylab B was canceled due to lack of funding. The module was put into storage, then donated to the National Air and Space Museum, where it remains on display.

APOLLO-SOYUZ

Apollo-Soyuz – Apollo Soyuz Test Project (ASTP) – was the first joint space mission between the United States and the Soviet Union. Although considered by some to be part of the original AAP, ATSP is perhaps more correctly seen as a part of the Integrated Program Plan, an ambitious, post AAP concept presented by NASA administrator Thomas Paine to the Nixon administration (see chapter 10). However, considering that the ATSP mission used a leftover Apollo command and service module launched by a surplus Saturn 1B, it can be seen as a de facto inclusion in AAP.

The mission was the last flight of the CSM, would be the last crewed U.S. spaceflight until 1981 when the first crewed Space Shuttle launched, and was the last crewed flight in a NASA-derived capsule. Apollo-Soyuz was also the first and only flight for Deke Slayton. Slayton was one of the original Mercury Seven but was medically suspended from astronaut service in 1962, remaining suspended until 1972. He was the oldest person to fly in space at the time.

Along with Slayton were astronauts Thomas Stafford and Vance Brand. When they docked with the Soyuz spacecraft they shook hands with cosmonauts Alexei Leonov and Valeri Kubasov. Apollo-Soyuz was Brand's first space flight as well. He would later command three shuttle missions. Stafford was a seasoned astronaut, and Leonov and Kubasov were experienced cosmonauts.

Both the U.S. Saturn 1B and the Soviet Soyuz-U launched on July 15, 1975 for the six day docked mission, although after separation of the respective capsules the CSM orbited three more days.

That the Apollo-Soyuz mission took place two and a half months after the end of the Vietnam War was significant. A joint U.S.-Soviet mission had been under consideration since 1970, even though Cold War tensions between the two nations were high. However, from the Soviet viewpoint in particular, such cooperation was off the table as long as U.S. involvement in Vietnam continued.

Still, behind the scenes American and Soviet engineers put aside differences and had been cooperating since 1971, working together to create compatible engineering, particularly regarding the docking module. That Apollo-Soyuz happened so quickly after the end of the war connotes how eager both sides were to make this international statement of cooperation and détente. Although both joint and separate science experiments were performed during the flight, and docking mechanisms for the International Space Station were initially developed, Apollo-Soyuz was largely a public relations event, the positive outcome of such relations welcomed by both nations. The mission is generally considered to be the end of the Space Race.

VOYAGER

In 1964 Gary Flandro of the Jet Propulsion Laboratory (JPL) realized that Jupiter, Saturn, Uranus, and Neptune would align in the late 1970s, a phenomenon that happens once every 175 years. He proposed a mission using a single spacecraft. The total mission time would be thirteen years. By 1966 JPL was promoting the idea.

In 1969 NASA's Outer Planets Working Group proposed using two spacecraft, calling the overall mission the Grand Tour. Using two spacecraft would halve the original timeline.

However, by 1971 the budget for the Grand Tour was nearing $1 billion (in 1971 dollars). The Space Shuttle had been approved by this time and needed funding. Plus, many in Congress grumbled about the expense and need of this cosmic (if nearby) undertaking. The Grand Tour was cancelled in late 1971. The mission would then reemerge in different forms.

Rather than being completely cancelled, the Grand Tour, and its concept based on planetary alignment, was downsized into to the two Voyager missions. Although unmanned, the Voyager missions can, in many ways, be considered the most successful component of what survived from AAP. The two probes completed a significant portion of the Grand Tour, at least in terms of proximity if not thoroughness. The probes remain active presently, continuing to relay data to Earth. Voyager 1, in 2022, was over 23 billion kilometers from the sun; Voyager 2, over 19 billion kilometers. Both probes have been successful beyond what anyone at JPL, or anywhere, might have dreamed.

Despite the numeration, Voyager 2 was launched first, August 20, 1977. From 1979 to 1989 the probe visited the Jovian system, the Saturnian system, the Uranian system, and the Neptunium system.

Voyager 1 was launched September 5, 1977. The probe was designed to move faster than Voyager 2, which is why Voyager 1 is presently significantly farther from the sun than its cousin. Voyager 1 made flybys of Jupiter, Saturn, and Saturn's largest moon, Titan. The Grand Tour would have included Pluto. Voyager 1's flight path could have included Pluto, but the decision was made to fly by Titan.

Voyager 2's nuclear battery was predicted to last until 2020, which it has surpassed. Voyager 1's battery is predicted to last until 2025. When the power sources are depleted the probes will continue on under Newton's first law. Both probes have crossed the boundary of the heliosphere (the edge of the solar wind) and have entered what is considered interstellar space.

As suggested, the LRV can be considered part of AAP. From the era of the *Collier's* articles von Braun envisioned moon landings to be expeditionary in scope, including pressurized vehicles for mobility, such vehicles being in the three- to four-ton range. During the early days of Apollo development two Saturn V launches were assumed for each mission. One to transport the astronauts and the lunar landing craft, another to transport the supplies and equipment for the astronauts to stay up to six weeks, and to transport roving vehicles.

By 1964 Apollo's budget was already being cut by Congress, making two-launch moon missions impossible. The

LM was originally called the LEM – lunar excursion module. But there would be no lengthy excursions now.

105

10

At more than half a century out now Apollo is so easily filed into history as a mission accomplished, not so much different from a completed dam or a new interstate road. We decided to do it and we did, story over. Actually, the same sentiment was true in 1979, just one decade out from the first lunar landing. But then even the 1979 date is not surprising. By the last Apollo flight in December of 1972 the impatient spectators had already left the stadium for their cars, game over.

In most popular histories of Apollo, even more scholarly works, that Apollo would end so often seems a given within the narrative. Again, Apollo is typically depicted, if implicitly, as a public works project that was completed. During the first five years or so of Apollo, however, within NASA and the space community, Apollo was seen as an adventure to begin, and to then continue.

The Apollo witnessed by the masses was not a project planned in toto in 1961, and then carried out without deviation. Nearly from the beginning the program was altered along the way, and was far more a result of what would work at a given stage of the project – not so much technically, but what would be considered by Congress, accepted by Congress, and what Congress would then fund. In fact today Apollo is defined far more by what might have happened but didn't than by what did. From the beginning ideas and concepts emerged, from back-of-the-envelope notes and sketches that never much evolved to by-the-book proposals, from within both NASA and the aerospace community.

Only a small fraction of AAP saw reality, and even those missions required a looser definition of AAP. (See chapter 9.) However, even as AAP was actively not happening, other initiatives, paradoxically, were emerging. These initiatives would continue to emerge periodically during the post-Apollo decades. Some, without surprise, were political theater, delivered with the knowledge that Congressional support and funding would never happen.

In the late 1960s, even as von Braun himself was accepting that Apollo would simply end without being finished, and that post-Apollo years would find anemic funding for manned spaceflight, others continued to push for a true space age to emerge in the 1970s.

Integrated Program Plan

For the most part separate from AAP, the Integrated Program Plan (IPP) emerged in 1969 under new NASA chief Thomas O. Paine, who succeeded James Webb. Whereas AAP was a potentially workable response to a political climate increasingly unfriendly to Apollo, IPP was a highly ambitious plan that, quite mistakenly, assumed a new and now ever increasing NASA budget.

Paine was a successful and well-regarded research scientist, and therefore scientifically trained. Webb was not scientifically trained, but before his time at NASA had gained extensive management skills in both private and government settings, mostly government at the Federal level. Paine lacked Webb's human insight and political skills, and perhaps was too logical for the job. He assumed that the obvious function of if-then statements was accepted generally. Such as *if* NASA has done such a tremendous job of carrying out a successful lunar landing program, *then* the agency deserves to be rewarded with a relatively free hand going forward across the next decade, and beyond. Of all that happens in Washington, then and now, the successful application of if-then statements was and is not overly common.

Paine held his position for just eighteen months. During that time he pushed IPP hard. His proposals would have turned the 1960s into a dress rehearsal compared to what he hoped the 1970s would bring. Not understanding well enough how Washington worked, Paine was unwilling to offer smaller versions of the overall plan – i.e., willing to select certain components over others – and he held to a timeline that was exceedingly optimistic, even had working cooperation and funding from the White House and Congress been forthcoming.

The IPP included these major goals:

- Permanent space stations in low Earth orbit, geosynchronous orbit, and lunar polar orbit

- Continued production of Saturn V and Saturn V-derived rockets

- The Space Transportation System (Space Shuttle)

- A space tug operable manned or unmanned and capable of lunar landing

- A nuclear-powered shuttle using the proposed NERVA nuclear-thermal rocket engine

- A mission to Mars

- Permanent lunar and then Mars bases

Despite von Braun's realistic viewpoint about Apollo and beyond, at Paine's request he appeared before the Space Task Group (STG) two weeks after the Apollo 11 landing to present a case for landing on Mars in the early 1980s. Vice President Spiro Agnew was chairman of STG and expressed enthusiasm about IPP, an enthusiasm that would not be imparted to Richard Nixon.

The cost of AAP was based on existing Apollo hardware, and part of the promoted appeal of AAP was to maximize the investment already made. The cost of IPP was unspecified, but it would have dwarfed the $25 billion total spent on Apollo.

Even before Paine began promoting IPP, the Nixon White House had stated not just that NASA's budget would decline, but that it would decline rapidly. Nixon, as an individual, found no visceral excitement in manned spaceflight, as Johnson did from the beginning and as Kennedy acquired. (Ironically, all Apollo lunar landings, and the accompanying prestige, would happen during Nixon's first administration.) Just as important, if not more so, Nixon also saw no political advantage in expanding manned space flight, or, really, even to continue manned space flight, with one exception, the Space Shuttle.

California was crucial to Nixon's 1972 re-election bid and California contractors were crucial to the Shuttle. Such contractors would, of course, create thousands of aerospace jobs. In addition, Caspar Weinberger, at the time deputy director of the Office of Management and Budget, suggested to Nixon that ending American manned spaceflight during his administration would tarnish his legacy. The Shuttle was the only part of Paine's plan that survived.

BEYOND 17: THE APOLLO APPLICATIONS PROGRAM AND LOSING THE NEW FRONTIER

In the original IPP plan the Shuttle was to deliver not only astronauts, but also cargo, and propellants for refueling in LEO. The Shuttle was basically a space pickup truck envisioned to service the other IPP components, but now it had no real destination beyond achieving orbit. Although the Shuttle would often carry a payload, it never carried workaday cargo or propellants. The last Shuttle flew in July 2011. After that date, the United States had no system to launch astronauts until the private SpaceX Dragon spacecraft launched in May 2020. In the interim NASA contracted with Roscosmos, the Russian space agency, to transport astronauts to the International Space Station.

***

The de facto end of Apollo in no way ended the speculative work of those in NASA, in the aerospace community, and in the scientific community; and in no way ended the hopes and dreams implicit to that work. Some of these specific hopes found reality, and spectacular success, in robotic exploration, including, from the 1970s, Pioneer 10, Pioneer 11, Viking 1, and Viking 2. And yet the sheer adventure and romance of human spaceflight, the existential accomplishment and reaffirmation of not deferring to machines, the actual seeing of distant creation with naked human eyes on site, all of these quests lived on. As Neil de Grasse Tyson once said, "Nobody's ever given a parade for a robot." And yet since Apollo, a schism has existed between politics and the actual nuts-and-bolts undertaking of grand audacity.

After resigning from NASA Paine returned to General Electric, later going to Northrop. However, he never stopped championing space exploration while he fulfilled his duties in private industry. In 1984 President Reagan, by executive order, commissioned a panel to evaluate the future of the nation's space program, appointing Paine chairman. In 1986 the panel issued their results, which included a significant amount of public input, gathered at hearings throughout the nation. *Pioneering the Space Frontier* promoted "a pioneering mission for 21st-century America … to lead the exploration and development of the space frontier, advancing science, technology, and enterprise, and building institutions and systems that make accessible vast new resources and support human settlements beyond Earth orbit, from the highlands of the Moon to the plains of Mars." As with previous and subsequent such reports, *Pioneering the Space Frontier* was all but ignored.

Also in 1984, Reagan approved Space Station Freedom, a large, permanently crewed craft. Although primarily a United States project, Space Station Freedom would have also involved the participation of the Canadian, Japanese, British, and European space agencies. Congress balked at the station's size and cost. The craft was redesigned seven times in ten years, each new design reducing size and functionality. By 1993, the station now within the purview of the Clinton administration, the project was politically untenable. Efforts were then aimed at incorporating the existing design work into the International Space Station.

In January 1988, President Reagan approved a revised U.S. space policy with the overall goal of expanding "human presence and activity beyond Earth orbit into the solar system." The policy was based in part on the 1987 Ride Report, formally titled *Leadership and America's Future in Space*. Former astronaut Sally Ride was chairman of the committee issuing the report. Among other goals, the report pushed for a permanent moon base in the first decade of the 2000s, followed by a manned Mars landing.

President George H. W. Bush's commemoration of the twentieth anniversary of Apollo 11 illustrated this schism more precisely. On July 20, 1989, Bush stood on the steps of the National Air and Space Museum to announce the Space Exploration Initiative (SEI). The Initiative included a permanent space station far more elaborate than Skylab; the Common Lunar Landing program, a series of mostly robotic missions to survey the lunar surface cartographically and geologically; a permanent lunar base; and the International Lunar Resource Exploration Concept, which would seek international cooperation – mostly from the Soviet Union – in establishing a larger lunar base and lunar logistics.

Encouraged by the speech, NASA administrator Richard Truly initiated the *Ninety-Day Study on Human Exploration of Moon and Mars* to explore fulfilling the SEI goals. The report was released in November 1989. Rather than an accelerated Apollo-like program with a specific date to accomplish the goal, the report envisioned, as in the very early days of Apollo, a quest to begin, and then continue. The initial missions would happen over at least twenty years, with a cost of $500 billion, twenty times the cost of Apollo (using unadjusted dollars).

Not surprisingly, the report was met in Congress with significant opposition, often to the extent of derision and hostility. Quoting Senator Jim Sasser of Tennessee, "The President took one giant leap for starry-eyed political rhetoric, and not even a small step for fiscal responsibility. The hard fact is, this Administration doesn't even have its space priorities established for next year, much less for the next century." Al Gore, at the time also a Senator from Tennessee, said "By proposing a return to the Moon, with no money, no timetable, and no plan, President Bush offers the country not a challenge to inspire us, but a daydream to briefly entertain us, a daydream about as splashy as a George Lucas movie, with about as much connection to reality."

SEI did not survive the transition to the Clinton administration, or the directives of Truly's successor Dan Goldin. But then painting Bill Clinton and Dan Goldin as the bad guys is too easy, and unfair.

When Truly's report was delivered not only did Congress balk at the cost, but, incredibly, so did the White House. The conclusion must be reached, then, that while someone wrote a motivating speech for President Bush, no one in the White House ran the numbers on such an undertaking. As well, concluding that Bush's presentation on the Air and Space steps was political theater – empty of any real commitment, or a way to pay for the initiative – is all but unavoidable.

Like any huge national and collective goal, a true age of space must be wanted viscerally and insistently at a significant level across the culture extant, including in Congress. Since December of 1972, at the very latest, that goal has not been wanted even simply, without the adverbs.

BEYOND 17: THE APOLLO APPLICATIONS PROGRAM AND LOSING THE NEW FRONTIER

A Long History of Speculative Design

Among engineers and designers, and fanciful thinkers, humans living in space, and on the moon and Mars, has been a potent idea since the time of Jules Verne, and later H.G. Wells. Then, beginning in the 1940s when space travel knowledge, application, theories, and hypotheses emerged in some technical practicality, ideas for space working and living have abounded. Here are just a few.

Let's start on a humorous note, although this proposal was offered seriously at the time, though not taken so. The proposal? A one-way trip to the moon. Kennedy's May 1961 address to Congress of course included not only landing a man on the moon by 1970, but also returning him to Earth safely.

But hold on, said John Cord and Leonard Seale. In 1962 Cord, an engineer at Bell Aerospace, and Seale, a Bell psychologist, figured beating the Soviets to the moon was paramount, and by beating the Soviets the pair meant getting an American on the moon. Getting him back safely could wait.

The Soviet space program was shrouded in secrecy. Missions were announced only after they were completed successfully. In 1962 the Soviets were demonstrably ahead of the U.S. in current space ventures, and the Soviet's capacity in space was assumed to be broad and growing, to the extent many thought a Soviet lunar landing could take place in 1965.

That assumption was wrong. The Soviets, assuming the U.S. was bluffing about a moonshot, didn't begin serious planning and execution for a lunar landing until 1964. But in 1962 a 1965 Soviet landing was the fear, and so Cord and Seale concocted their plan.

Remotely controlled unmanned cargo capsules with supplies would be in place near the lunar landing zone when the lone astronaut landed. Other cargo capsules would land periodically. The supplies would allow a stay of up to twenty-four months.

Cord and Seale utilized the direct ascent mode in their plan. Since the first lunar landing craft would not need propellant to launch from the moon, and the CSM capsule would not need parachutes or a heat shield to reenter Earth's atmosphere, the overall weight would be cut very significantly, and the mission could be launched by a modified and enhanced Saturn I (the Saturn V was still under development).

The mission was extremely dangerous. Once injected into a lunar path the astronaut could not abort, either due to system failure or an external environmental event. Radiation would be a problem, since a shield would add too much weight. Solar flares could also have been a problem, not to mention the isolation.

The first full Apollo mission would then return the first man on the moon to Earth in one piece, at least physically. The condition the lone astronaut might have been in above the neck could have been another story. NASA declined this method.

The Chrysler automobile company we know today (now owned by Stellantis, a multinational holding company headquartered in Amsterdam) is but a distant cousin to what Walter Chrysler's company once was. Chrysler had been known for fundamental innovation, including radios in cars, sealed beam headlights, the first overhead-valve high-compression V8, torsion bar suspension, and developing turbine engines for cars. In the beginning years of the Space Race Chrysler manufactured the first stage of the Saturn 1B. The company was at that time already in the missile building business.

EVAs – spacewalks outside a spacecraft – were at first surprisingly uncertain. In mid-1965, cosmonaut Alexei Leonov was the first spacewalker, followed by astronaut Ed White one month later. Both experienced problems, including overheated pressure suits, difficulty of control, and, in White's case, anyway, ballooning of the pressure suit. Both men had difficulty reentering their capsules. Today spacewalks outside the International Space Station are routine.

By the time Leonov and White walked in space, Chrysler engineers Edsel Dunford and R. Dutzmann were already working on a way to better protect exposed astronauts in their nylon pressure suits. They assumed, however speculatively, that the time following the early Apollo years would be one of expanding space exploration, and that exteriors of spacecraft, and exterior components such as radio dishes, would require maintenance and repair by astronauts. They saw potential problems with meteorites, radiation, and the basic logistics of handling tools and materials.

They designed an independently flying platform that looked pretty much like a round phone booth. Von Braun had imagined such a craft earlier, but one sealed and pressurized with mechanical manipulating arms. Dunford and Dutzmann figured astronauts would need to perform their exterior duties hands on, or rather gloved-hands on. From their perspective mechanical arms with pincers as crude hands was too clumsy.

Their craft, the Transportation and Work Station Capsule, was open to space, allowing astronauts to lean out to put their hands on their work. The capsule was sort of like a bucket truck in space.

Tools could be kept in the capsule, rather than on a belt worn by a free-floating astronaut. The capsule was sealable in an emergency, in particular a damaged and leaking pressure suit, and had a backup oxygen supply.

The fundamental purpose of Apollo was, of course, exploration. But lunar exploration would always be in limiting pressure suits, and the first three successful landings (Apollo 13 didn't land, obviously) would involve exploration by walking. Apollo 15, 16, and 17 carried lunar roving vehicles (LRV), but even then walking was a key factor. Astronauts could not drive the LRV any distance beyond that which could be walked to return to the LM should the LRV break down.

Like any hiker, the astronauts carried backpacks. These backpacks held a rechargeable electrical system, air for breathing, and water for cooling their bodies. All three consumables were crucial, and time was the governing factor.

Responding to these limits, in July of 1967 planners recommended the development of a Lunar Flying Unit (LFU) to increase astronaut mobility on the moon. The LFU would have a range of up to ten kilometers. They hoped the LFU might be ready for the last Apollo missions, 18, 19, and 20, from the perspective of 1967. If not, then the LFU would be ready for AAP.

The recommendation came about two weeks before Congress slashed NASA's budget as a response to the Apollo 1 fire. Although the fire happened in January, and the flight schedule was on hold, at the time LFU proponents still remained optimistic about AAP.

Two contractors were involved in the design of the LFU, Bell Aerospace and North American Rockwell. Bell's design was a flying platform with four landing legs. The pilot stood in a three-sided enclosure.

The pilot in Rockwell's design would sit upright and slightly forward. This position lowered the center of mass significantly, compared to standing, and so improved stability. The Rockwell design was innovative, but more complex than Bell's design, plus it had a shorter range.

Both designs had their quirks. While the Bell design placed the engine exhaust on either side of the pilot, Rockwell's design placed the engines under the platform, which would kick up lunar debris directly around the astronaut pilot. This required dragging the unit onto a fabric pad for launching. Unlike Bell's design, Rockwell's had shock absorbers, which was good because Rockwell engineers suggested shutting the engine down at some distance above the landing site to reduce scattering debris. (Bell's shock absorbers were the human knee, the same shock absorbers used in the LM.) Bell's LFU wouldn't continue flying if an engine failed, but Rockwell's would. With an added propellant package, Bell claimed its LFU could reach lunar orbit. In an emergency, Rockwell's unit could reach just several hundred feet in altitude. Curiously, the early Bell LFUs would be fueled from leftover descent fuel in the LM. Experience would show leftover fuel could not be assumed.

Utilizing upgraded engines Bell also envisioned its unit becoming a Mars Flying Unit.

Bell Aerospace and North American Rockwell submitted their final reports in May 1969 just as the Marshall Space Flight Center announced focus would be on the LRV. Boeing was selected as the prime contractor for the LRV.

These are only a few of the hundreds of concepts and proposals that came from NASA and contractors both. For most of the 1960s aerospace engineers saw Apollo as a program that would grow across the 1970s, and then beyond. Understandably they let their imaginations roam trying to anticipate what tools and devices would be needed in a future of humans living and working beyond Earth.

11

There was an 800-pound gorilla[13] in the room of the Apollo era. That furry simian was both the war in Vietnam and Johnson's Great Society program.

The hearts and minds of Americans, reflecting Eisenhower's lament, were largely unchanged in the post-war years, both in the populace and in leadership. Just five years after the end of World War II, the Korean War erupted. Korea, after liberation from Japan at the end of the World War II, was divided north and south into occupation zones, the north Soviet controlled, the south U.S. controlled. The division was to be temporary, but Cold War tensions continued the divide.

In June of 1950 North Korean forces crossed the divide, the infamous 38th parallel, invading South Korea. The war was essentially a proxy war between the Soviet Union allied with China, and the U.S. and its allies. From many points of view, the U.S. had little choice but to respond to the invasion. The three-year conflict was fought to a stalemate, ending in 1953. Korea remains divided to this day. The next year, the U.S. sent the first advisors to South Vietnam.

The full-scale war that would emerge in Vietnam was also a proxy war, with the same players respectively, north and south. However, U.S. participation in Vietnam was far less denoted compared to the U.S. response to the invasion of South Korea.

The war in Vietnam resulted in stark irony for Kennedy and Johnson regarding their mutual support of the space program. The war's drain on the federal budget, along with the

Apollo 1 fire, provided Congress with reasons to cut the Apollo budget, eventually eliminating the project.

The French had ruled Vietnam as a colony since 1887, although a European presence had been in Vietnam for centuries. The conflict between the French and the Viet Min emerged from the First Indochina War, which began in 1946. In 1954 France withdrew its military forces from Vietnam. At that time the nation was then divided into north and south entities.

As the French withdrew, the United States assumed financial and military support of South Vietnam during the Eisenhower years. The military support was virtually all hardware and financial aid. By the end of Eisenhower's second term less than 1,000 American military advisors were in country. (Military advisors were soldiers typically from the U.S. Army Special Forces and the Marines. By definition their roles were advisory and non-combatant.)

For the most part, Kennedy continued the Cold War policy begun by Harry Truman and carried on by Eisenhower. Faced with the Bay of Pigs failure, the construction of the Berlin Wall, and the Cuban Missile Crisis Kennedy was compelled to show strength against communist expansion. After his disastrous 1961 meeting with Khrushchev in Vienna he told James Reston, in a *New York Times* interview, "Now we have a problem making our power credible and Vietnam looks like the place." Kennedy began increasing American presence dramatically, to the extent that by 1964 23,000 military advisors were in Vietnam.

In August of 1964, the Gulf of Tonkin incident took place. The incident was a clash between the USS *Maddox,* on a covert mission, and North Vietnamese torpedo boats. The event was inflated and fabricated into a definitive reason for even greater U.S. involvement. The Gulf of Tonkin Resolution passed by Congress gave Johnson extensive authority to increase the U.S. military presence, even though a formal declaration of war was not made. Johnson deployed the first combat troops, which would quickly reach 184,000. By 1967 U.S. troop presence reached 475,000.

At the beginning of his first administration Richard Nixon began a program of shifting actual combat activity to the South Vietnamese forces. By early 1973, under agreements contained in the Paris Peace Accords, remaining U.S. ground forces had been withdrawn, leaving South Vietnam to defend itself with its own troops. However, U.S. air support, artillery support, material support, advisor support, and direct aid to the South Vietnamese government continued, as did the drain on the treasury by the many billions per year. (To review, the total cost of Apollo was about $25 billion. The total cost of the war in Vietnam was about $168 billion; about $140 billion was spent on the war during the time of Apollo.)

Despite the peace accords, the war in Vietnam continued another two years. In 1974 Congress ended all military aid to South Vietnam. Without U.S. air support South Vietnam was unable to defend itself. The conflict ceased on April 30, 1975, simply because on that date North Vietnamese forces overran and captured Saigon, the South Vietnamese capital.

From our current perspective U.S. involvement in Vietnam was a massive mistake. Indeed, that conclusion was reached rather definitively by the late 1970s. We can only conjecture what Kennedy and then Johnson might have done alternatively. However, we must acknowledge that both men sowed seeds that were partially responsible for undoing the Apollo vision held by each.

In addition to the war in Vietnam, Johnson's Great Society initiative was also a major drain on the treasury. Since Johnson wanted to implement the initiative while staying within yearly budgets part of the funding had to be diverted from elsewhere, including Apollo and so AAP.

The Great Society, in part, continued stalled aspects of Kennedy's New Frontier. The Great Society was a highly ambitious program with the fundamental goal of eliminating poverty and racial injustice. Such lofty goals were noble and just.

However, again we must conjecture, in this case about a possible earlier and so longer path that would have made such a concentrated level of spending unnecessary. Our post-war behavior did not acknowledge the apprehensions of Eisenhower, or the hopes of a better world realized through new thinking and awareness.

The American effort in World War II saw a significant participation by women and minorities. Women were in the military directly, and in war related domestic work and manufacturing forces. Black, Hispanic, and Native American men, along with other minorities, served in all branches of the military. Many Rosie the Riveters were black women.

And yet the post-war years held a subjugation of all women. Those years also held little acknowledgement of the contributions made by minority soldiers who fought for their country. In the South many tried to reclaim an ante bellum past, keeping hundreds of thousands of black families in poverty, often abject. For that matter, if to an obviously lesser degree, the same can be said for many white southern families. To varying degrees, black families were suppressed in most any geographic location.

What if, somehow, we had experienced an epiphany? What if leaders in those early post-war years had led with true vision and inspiration? What if there had been no political room for the likes of Joseph McCarthy? What if in the post-war years all workers had received a living wage? What if minorities had been accepted into the culture extant? What if women had been seen as whole human beings with hopes and dreams? Perhaps then the costs of righting inequities would have been not only less, but spread over decades, thus not requiring a diversion of funds from programs like Apollo.

Well, *what ifs* are easy to fire off. In reality, as noted in chapter three, the seminal times of technologies and cultural movements happen years and decades before such developments enter the popular consciousness. We can only surmise, then, that the seeds of Congressional shortsightedness and of the public mendacity of 1972 that held the dismissal of Apollo 17 had been planted in those earlier, first post-war years.

***

Just as the initial U.S. involvement in Vietnam was a carryover from the 1940s, at least in terms of the Cold War that resulted from World War II, much of the cultural 1950s looked like the 1940s. Women wore flouncy dresses, and hats atop bouncy hairdos. Men wore elaborate suits with pleated pants and wide ties. And hats atop very short hair. Colonial and traditional houses continued to be built, and the domesticity within those houses continued to emphasize the nuclear family and an idealized past. Still, on some facets there was significantly more to the 1950s than an anachronistic gestalt with the goal of returning to life as it was in the pre-war years.

In 1954 the U.S. Supreme Court, issuing a landmark decision in the case of *Brown v. Board of Education of Topeka*, ruled that segregation in public schools was unconstitutional. The decision among the justices was unanimous. The case was seminal in the quest for equal rights.

Ten years earlier, with remarkable foresight, Congress passed the Serviceman's Readjustment Act of 1944, better known as the G.I. Bill. Available to virtually all honorably discharged World War II veterans, the bill provided low-cost mortgages and business loans, plus tuition payments and living expenses for servicemen who wanted to attend college, or take advantage of other educational opportunities.

The original G.I. Bill expired in 1956, although the term has been used casually since then to describe other legislation to benefit veterans. By 1956, almost eight million G.I.s had used the educational benefits, over two million of those attending college. The G. I. Bill was both a considered breaking with the past and a calculated grabbing of The Future. Sadly, such a break was not complete enough, in that minority veterans very often were prevented from accessing their full benefits.

Later social change would see the hippie counterculture era of the 1960s and 1970s, which can be traced to the beatniks of the previous generation. In that era, social demand for racial equality intensified, as did an emerging push for gender equality, and an emerging concern for the environment, as well as an intense protest against the war in Vietnam.

The post-war years in military aviation saw the rise of jet fighters, as well as, in 1952, the groundbreaking B-52 bomber (which, remarkably, remains in service). Nineteen fifty-two also saw the debut of commercial jet aviation with the British de Haviland Comet. The Comet was plagued by metal fatigue, which led to an inauspicious start. Then in 1958, the Boeing 707 first saw commercial use. The 707 would soon find widespread use, dominating the 1960s in not only passenger service, but in cargo and military applications as well. Even to the casual observer a jet-powered commercial airliner, with its swept back wings and lack of propellers, was a hallmark of The Future. The 707 is credited with beginning the Jet Age.

Automobile design moved ahead slowly in the 1950s, with the exception of the 1953 Chevrolet Corvette and the 1953 Studebaker Commander. Both models were a radical break from the past and both suggested the Space Age to come. The man in space articles in *Collier's* magazine began running the previous year, and the serious notion of manned space travel existed, if esoterically, among a few visionaries in government and within the aerospace industry.

In addition to some emerging social changes, more to the point in the 1950s The Future emerged in architecture, that architecture being public, observable evidence to all.

The United Nations Secretariat Building, completed in 1951, was a total departure from the stone-clad skyscrapers to date, utilizing the glass curtain wall design that would become emblematic of post-war construction. Lever House followed in

1952, headquarters for Lever Brothers. The Seagram Building, completed in 1958, quickly became one of the most iconic International Style buildings in the American landscape, with Mies van der Rohe as principal architect. All three buildings are located in Manhattan. Although the Empire State Building and the Chrysler Building contained movement towards modernity in their designs, buildings designed in the International Style created a clear watershed indicating forward movement – The Future – within a conservative culture.

The International style had been around since the 1920s, mostly in Europe. The earliest example in the United States was the PSFS building in Philadelphia, completed in 1932. However, both the Boley Building in Kansas City, designed by Louis Curtiss and completed in 1909, and the Hallidie Building in San Francisco, designed by Willis Polk and completed in 1918, were earlier examples of the glass curtain wall, and were precursors of the International Style.

American architecture in the first two decades of the twentieth century was a carryover from the nineteenth century, as was a significant amount of fashion and culture, and so both the Boley Building and the Hallidie Building were stark demarcations, hinting of The Future even then. However, neither was a skyscraper and both were adorned with classical decoration, leaving the United Nations building as the seminal structure. The International Style did not really flourish in the United States until after 1950. The International Style *was* modernity.

Frank Lloyd Wright also pursued The Future with his designs. His Usonian designs, which were affordable alternatives to traditional housing, were house designs completely apart from traditional architecture in both design and materials. The designs were open, reflecting the needs of the modern family. They were designed to blur the border between interior living and nature, and to engender a new perspective, a new way of thought. Although many were built in the late 1930s and the first part of the 1940s, most were constructed across the 1950s.

Wright also designed the Guggenheim Museum in New York. Construction began in 1956 with completion in 1959. The museum was to showcase non-objective art. Wright, then, designed what could be called a non-objective building, in that, although it was clearly a structure of some sort, it looked like no other building in Manhattan. Or anywhere. The Guggenheim looked like what Wright intended. It looked like The Future.

From the street the main section of the museum looks like the top of a truncated graduated cone. This section is the actual gallery, a continuous spiral rising six stories.

The Guggenheim was built just a few blocks from the Metropolitan Museum of Art, which was designed in the Beaux-Arts style. Wright described the Met as a "Protestant barn" and a "coffin for the spirit." He wanted to shake up the establishment. He did. The art critic for the *New York Times* called the Guggenheim "a war between architecture and painting in which both come out badly maimed." Amidst the clunky cars and the flouncy dresses and the pleated pants – amidst the *Ozzie and Harriet* of it all – Wright's design screamed The Future.

Two years before the Guggenheim opened construction began on two buildings that would push beyond modernity. The Theme Building at Los Angeles International Airport (LAX), and the TWA terminal at the John F. Kennedy International Airport (JFK) in New York.

The Theme Building, designed by Paul Williams and Welton Beckett of Pereira and Luckman Architects, looks like a just-landed UFO. A pair of arches intersect at 90°. Below, in faux suspension, is the saucer containing the interior space of the structure.

The original plan for LAX, also by Pereira and Luckman, envisioned all terminals and parking structures connected to a huge glass dome, which would have served as a distribution hub for passenger foot traffic. That plan was scuttled. The Theme Building was constructed on the site where the glass dome would have been centered.

Beyond even the LAX Theme Building in chasing The Future, however, was the fantastic TWA terminal at JFK (at the time called New York International Airport, commonly known as Idlewild Airport). Designed by Eero Saarinen, the building was completed in 1962. The swooping, undulating building is a collection of organic forms, outside and in. Except for utilitarian components such as stair steps, railings, and service hallways, finding 90° angles is a challenge. Even after sixty years, the building is a perfect backdrop for a sci-fi story. Thankfully, in the early 2000s negotiations saved the central part of the building from demolition. Saarinen also designed the futuristic terminal at Dulles International Airport in Washington, D.C., completed in 1963.

BEYOND 17: THE APOLLO APPLICATIONS PROGRAM AND LOSING THE NEW FRONTIER

Compare the LAX Theme Building or the JFK TWA terminal or the Dulles terminal – three such forward looking, forward thinking, forward moving buildings from the late 1950s and early 1960s – with later buildings, particularly of the postmodern style. Postmodernism was a reaction/response to the International Style and the form-follows-function implicit to that style. Postmodernism saw the reintroduction of decoration.

The AT&T building in New York, now known as 550 Madison Avenue, completed in 1984, is seen as the first postmodern skyscraper. The top of the thirty-seven story building is a giant broken pediment. The AT&T building was codesigned by Philip Johnson, along with John Burgee. Ironically, Johnson also codesigned the Seagram Building, along with Mies van der Rohe.

Johnson and Burgee also designed PPG Place in Pittsburgh, which can be described as a forty-story glass cathedral. The root word of *cathedral* is *cathedra*, the official throne of a bishop. A cathedral is the building in which the bishop's throne sits. But then American cathedrals, if in their de facto and egalitarian and bishop-less expressions, take other forms, such as the VAB, or the Saturn V itself.

Michael Graves was the most prolific architect of postmodernism, designing hundreds of buildings. His commercial buildings are clad in stone or concrete slabs and are fortress-like, as compared to the openness of the International Style. More anachronistic than postmodernism is New Classicism, which has seen, among other styles, buildings that are facsimiles of Greek and Roman temples. And so conversely to The Future is The Past.

Describing postmodernism as fortress-like is not inaccurate, and fortresses were not what the New Frontier was about. Postmodernism can be seen, again as observable evidence to all, as a rejection of The Future. That postmodernism emerged in earnest in the 1980s is not surprising.

As the International Style moved into the 1960s it was criticized for its austerity and sameness. The criticism was not unfounded, although such simplicity and uniformity emphasized that the ideas happening inside these buildings could be more important than the building itself. While postmodern buildings suggest explicitly the culture within, International Style buildings await implicitly out-of-the box thinking and creativity. While not directly linked with the International Style in evolution, the fantastic, Future-grabbing architecture of Dubai, Kuwait City, Jakarta, Kuala Lumpur, and in many cities across China, and to lesser degrees in New York, Moscow, London and other places, has a clear similarity to the International Style in materials and vision.

Of the iconic photos that capture the New Frontier – instantly and with no analysis needed – perhaps *Earthrise* is number one. Or maybe the photo of Buzz Aldrin on the moon, with a small reflection of Neil Armstrong in Aldrin's gold-coated visor. Standing at some distance in front of Aldrin, Armstrong took the photo, and so his own reflection. But those photos were taken at what would be the end of the New Frontier. In the case of the Aldrin image, the very end.

However, a central thesis of this book has been a wondering about this New Frontier, wondering about the outcomes had that vision taken root and continued. What about an iconic photo taken at the very start of the New Frontier? I didn't need to spend much time thinking about what that image might be. The image is not of rockets or astronauts in pressure suits, but of this modern architecture continuing to emerge.

In 1945, *Arts & Architecture* magazine commissioned major architects of the day, in particular forward-looking architects, to design and build inexpensive and efficient model homes that might meet the housing demand emerging after World War II. The resulting designs were not bungalows in a traditional style. No Cape Cods or saltboxes or haciendas. No wainscoting or quoins or broken pediments. These were midcentury designs, or to use a more general description, modern. Lots of glass. In many cases steel beams replaced wood.

In terms of popular accessibility, post-war architecture, in residential design and especially commercial design, defined the modern American scene more than any other art form or social vector. Far more than fashion or popular cultural tastes. Far more than automotive design or most of consumer industrial design. The post-war hopes of somehow avoiding another such war, of dragging a wrought, more peaceful future into reality, were displayed in these houses, many of which became homes.

These designs were known as the Case Study Houses. The program ran discontinuously until 1966. Not all designs saw construction.

The most famous Case Study House is #22, the Stahl house, designed by Pierre Koenig. Even if you've never heard of the Case Study series you've likely seen Julius Shulman's famous photo of the Stahl house. Entitled "Two Girls," the photo is considered one of the most influential of all time.

And why not? The house embodies the West, both geographically and culturally within the United States, and in cultural meaning globally. It sits on a near promontory in the Santa Monica mountains northwest of downtown Los Angeles, Sunset Boulevard below, at night the grid pattern of the city outlined in lights.

The front of the Stahl house, the public side, is windowless corrugated metal. Except for one short wall between the carport and a bedroom, and an exterior bathroom wall, the rest of the house is glass, top-to-bottom, side-to-side. The house was a rebuttal to the traditions and often puritanical morés of the East. The glass expanse loosened notions of inside and outside. Case Study House #22 became a home in which life was lived differently, in which the past was not so venerated.

Buck and Carlotta Stahl built the house. Two of their children cowrote *The Stahl House, Case Study House #22, The Making of a Modernist Icon*, published in 2021. In the book are dozens of family photos showing that different life – so casual, so informal, almost native. The house has a flat roof with very wide overhangs. The pool is very close to the house. My favorite photos show the Stahl children jumping off the roof into the pool, even as the Little Lord Fauntleroys back in the East were having their junior jodhpurs fitted. I can only think that today an uptight neighbor might call child protective services about these free-flying (and device-free) children.

To quote Julius Shulman, "What good is a dream house if you haven't got a dream?" The Stahls had a dream. They were not wealthy. From their apartment near the foot of Hollywood

Hills they could see the mountain jut that held the lot. "Our lot," they would say. The view was spectacular, and Buck determined to build on it.

The two drove up to their lot one day and, with delightful serendipity, came across the owner. With a handshake they negotiated a deal right then, walking away with a four year mortgage the developer carried personally. No construction could begin until the mortgage was paid.

Construction did begin in 1960, near the start of the New Frontier. The house became a monument to looking forward, to new thinking, to a new approach. It was, and still is, utterly emblematic of the New Frontier.

Such forward movement was also exhibited in other areas of the arts, including painting and graphic design, literature, film, and music. Painters such as Jasper Johns, Andy Warhol, and Roy Lichtenstein, to name only a few, challenged traditional morés of visual art. Writers Jack Kerouac, Allen Ginsberg, and William Burroughs – again, naming only a few of many – breached the limits of acceptability.

Amid the Technicolor treacle coming out of Hollywood in the 1950s were black-and-white American films that challenged happily ever after. Within that list are *Night of the Hunter, Beat the Devil, Touch of Evil, Baby Doll,* and *Ace in the Hole.*

Focusing on music, Elvis Presley made his first appearance on *The Ed Sullivan Show.* The appearance was not Presly's first television spot, having appeared earlier on The *Steve Allen Show* and *The Milton Berle Show.* Sullivan, in fact, did not want Presley on his show, but eventually agreed to three performances. The first, September 9, 1956, captured 60 million viewers, a whopping 82% of the viewing public. After the third performance Sullivan called Presley "a real decent, fine boy."

Due to his phenomenal, meteoric rise Presley, in particular, became emblematic of rock and roll, a genre of music with initial roots in the black culture of the '20s that began to emerge popularly in the late '40s. Others, of course, emerged with Presley, including Chuck Berry, Bill Haley, Little Richard, and Buddy Holly, among many, many others. (At this point those who would become The Beatles were just emerging in Liverpool.) By the very nature of rock and roll not being The Past, evidenced by the shock of the status quo, the music was in The Future.

In the end Apollo was an American original, as was jazz. In specific an African-American original, by 1950 or so earlier jazz had morphed into cool jazz, then later in the '50s modal jazz emerged. Art Blakey, Miles Davis, Thelonious Monk, and Stan Getz are among the best known from the era.

John Coltrane's 1961 cover of "My Favorite Things," the original a smarmy song oozing whiteness, was recorded at the same time Apollo was getting going. The piece is a soundtrack for the New Frontier, wonderfully emblematic of a parallax shift, beautiful in its juxtaposition – perhaps collision – of traditional music with jazz theory. That Coltrane, along with McCoy Tyner, Steve Davis, and Elvin Jones, distilled this take from the original arrangement was genius.

In 1959, as the idea of Apollo emerged in earnest, jazz greats Charles Mingus and Dave Brubeck each released seminal albums, Mingus's *Mingus Ah Um* and Brubeck's *Time Out*. In particular Brubeck's radical time signatures were a head-on collision with the moon-June-spoon songs that had come out of the Brill Building for years. Both album covers were created by S. Neil Fujita in the abstract expressionism style, so fitting to the music of the albums and to the times.

In that year The *Billboard* Top 100 songs included the usuals – Bobby Darin, Paul Anka, Connie Francis, Ricky Nelson, the Everly Brothers, and so on. At #67 was "The Chipmunk Song (Christmas Don't be Late)" sung by cartoon rodents. At #97 was the Mormon Tabernacle Choir's cover of "The Battle Hymn of the Republic." Rockin', baby. Then in 1961 Columbia released "Take Five" from *Time Out* as a single. The piece, written by saxophonist Paul Desmond, was a surprise hit. It reached the #97 position and remains the best-selling jazz single ever. Quoting Steve Race from the original liner notes, "In short: *Time Out* is a first experiment with time, which may well come to be regarded as more than an arrow pointing to the future. Something great has been attempted ... and achieved. The very first arrow has found its mark."

Returning to Kennedy's New Frontier speech (his 1960 acceptance speech as Democratic candidate), he said, "But the New Frontier of which I speak is not a set of promises – but a set of challenges. It sums up not what I intend to *offer* the American people, but what I intend to *ask* of them."

Ted Sorenson, an advisor to Kennedy who also wrote or helped draft many of Kennedy's speeches, wrote in his 2008 book *Ted Sorensen, Counselor: A Life at the Edge of History*, "American citizens today are filled with cynicism and distrust about presidential politics; most young people today assume that all modern presidents have deceived or disappointed the

American people. Perhaps it is worth reminding them that it is possible to have a president who is honest, idealistic, and devoted to the best values of this country. It happened at least once – I was there." Cultural historian Morris Dickstein has noted, "What we in hindsight call change is usually the unexpected swelling of a minor current as it imperceptibly becomes a major one and alters the prevailing mood."

And so, while small against the status quo, there were indeed post-war movements that aimed for a different future, perhaps even The Future. That aimed for an age of space, and a frontier new beyond what most had ever imagined. Across the spectrum of post-war American life, seeds of vision and imagination were sown, seeds to grow The Future. They were scattered across the popular culture landscape broadly, but the collective mass of these movements was ultimately too small to bring about epiphany in the culture extant, choked out by the weeds that grew from the seeds of complacency, seeds both political and cultural in origin.

In his speech, Kennedy quoted Winston Churchill from twenty years earlier. "If we open a quarrel between the present and the past, we shall be in danger of losing the future." Then Kennedy said, "Today our concern must be with that future. The old era is ending. The old ways will not do." More than six decades later, they still won't.

PART 2

Was there a New Frontier out there, somewhere?

139

12

After the first moon landing a cliché emerged within the popular vernacular. "If we can put a man on the moon why can't we _____?" Typically the blank was filled in with *eliminate poverty* or *end war* or *cure cancer*. In the broadest sense the question was fair. With not too much further consideration, though, the question and the usual fill-ins for the blank become apples and oranges.

Consider that a small maneuvering rocket engine under development, left sitting on a lab bench Friday afternoon, was unchanged when the technician returned Monday morning. For a social worker trying to alleviate poverty the same cannot be said for an impoverished family that is part of the caseload. Because mechanical dynamics and human dynamics are fundamentally different, both explicitly and implicitly, the social worker can in no way expect the Monday morning visit to reflect the state of the family in question as observed on the previous Friday afternoon.

Likewise with warfare, which can be quantified in a cursory way, but is still based, ultimately, on emotional states and visceral existentialism. The League of Nations was formed after World War I with the intent of preventing warfare. The subsequent founding of the United Nations immediately after World War II is evidence enough of the ineffectiveness of the League of Nations.

The basic premise of the League of Nations, and of the United Nations, was/is not so much to quantify conflict among nations, but to generally identify and compartmentalize conflict into forms receptive to negotiation and diplomacy. Although the United Nations has seen specific accomplishments at the humanitarian level dealing with famine and disaster, as well as providing healthcare and basic education on many facets, a quick look at headlines innumerable times over the last eighty years or so is again evidence enough that nations united in dialogue is rarely a cure for war, or certainly not often enough. People acting like people is often a slippery grab, one that just as often leads quickly to a slippery slope.

Even cancer outpaces soon enough the relative stasis of basic physics and chemistry as compared to biology. In theory biology can be reduced to physics and chemistry, and since Watson and Crick, in particular, has been to a significant degree. Still, in reality, if only due to the number of variables, biology can also be a slippery grab. People behave irrationally, exposing themselves to carcinogens by choice. Corporations create carcinogenic environments in pursuit of profit. (Seeking endless profit of staggering proportions is about power, and power, beyond what is needed to survive and to have basic comfort, is based in emotions, in that visceral existentialism.) In addition, even in the most basic biological research the contents of a petri dish change over the weekend.

Still, the initial question was a fair question, however broadly asked. Even during the time of Apollo few Americans had little understanding and appreciation for what was being accomplished. Few Americans had, and very few now have, a sense of the dedication and cooperation among the myriad of agencies and corporations that made Apollo happen. More so today than yesterday, many Americans don't even care that they don't know.

Time and again in the history of Apollo, what emerges is a dedication to a cause, a selflessness that today can seem anachronistic and quaint. In the earlier days of Apollo could be found, if esoterically, a genuine philosophy about what we were pursuing. The idea that moving out into space, beginning with Apollo, would change the very nature of humanity for the better. Regarding lofty goals of human hope and compassion, Apollo was and remains evidence – observable fact – that the impossible isn't.

Human dynamics – ambition, pride, emotions – were of course part of Apollo, to varying degrees across the spectrum of the 400,000 people who made 7-20-69 possible, simply because they were people. And yet that selflessness was the bow of Apollo, cutting through difficult times, chopping through the impossible. Four hundred thousand people who, for the most part, were both willing and wanting to be led. Of course von Braun was an excellent engineer and a technical visionary, but he was also an intuitive manager of people, to the extent of perceiving the psychology of an individual. His understanding of people might have been nearly as important as his understanding of rockets, regarding Apollo's success.

The same could be said for James Webb. Webb came from a progressive background and was instilled with an appreciation of active learning. Not simply learning inviolable fact and method, but understanding learning as an ongoing, self-correcting process. He was eager for Apollo to spark a permanent curiosity about *next* among the populace, so many of whom seemed mired in *back then*.

This positive, forward-looking view of humanity was not new. After World War II a vision emerged, or at least an active hope, that surely humanity could do better and must do better.

World War II saw horrific, unspeakable industrial killing. That war erupted barely more than two decades after the end of World War I, which was then known as the Great War, the war to end all wars. Another like conflict was needed to start numbering them.

In his book *The War That Will End War*, published early in World War I, H. G. Wells took the position that humanity and the planet could not endure another such war. World War I was the first truly mechanized war, made possible through advancing design and manufacture. It was also the first chemical war, and the first truly airborne war. The book's title was soon a catchphrase, one of idealism and hope for Wells. However, it became sardonic even before the war ended. Today the phrase is often used sarcastically.[14]

Before becoming the thirty-fourth president, Dwight Eisenhower was the Supreme Commander of the Allied Expeditionary Forces in World War II. In a speech given on April 16, 1953 he said, "Every gun made, every warship launched, every rocket fired signifies in the final sense, a theft from those who hunger and are not fed, those who are cold and are not clothed. This world in arms is not spending money alone. It is spending the sweat of its laborers, the genius of its scientists, the hopes of its children. The cost of one modern heavy bomber is this: a modern brick school in more than thirty cities. It is two electric power plants, each serving a town of sixty thousand in population. It is two fine, fully equipped hospitals. It is some fifty miles of concrete pavement. We pay for a single fighter with a half million bushels of wheat. We pay for a single destroyer with new homes that could house eight thousand people. This is not a way of life at all, in any true sense. Under the clouds of war, it is humanity hanging from a cross of iron."

Despite being a career soldier – or because of – Eisenhower also said, "I hate war as only a soldier who has lived it can, only as one who has seen its brutality, its futility, its stupidity." For that reason he insisted, in 1958, that NASA be created as a civilian agency, unbeholden to the military, as the Soviet space program very much was. Near the end of his second term he warned about the military industrial complex gaining unwarranted influence.

Eisenhower's many quotes about war, and, even as a five-star general, his acute apprehension about military power, particularly unsubordinated military power, indicated strongly his bewilderment about the primal and ongoing states of humanity that lead to war. He concluded, "We will bankrupt ourselves in the vain search for absolute security."

Between World War I and World War II, General Smedley D. Butler, of the Marines, published a short book, *War Is a Racket*. In his book Smedley focuses on who profits from and who pays for war. "A racket is best described, I believe," Butler wrote, "as something that is not what it seems to the majority of people. Only a small 'inside' group knows what it is about. It is conducted for the benefit of the very few, at the expense of the very many. Out of war a few people make huge fortunes."

Denis Diderot was a French philosopher from the Age of Enlightenment. In 1751 Diderot co-created the *Encyclopédie*. The work included articles skeptical about Biblical miracles. It was banned by the Catholic Church in 1758, by the French government in 1759. Diderot is probably best known for the quote, "Man will never be free until the last king is strangled with the entrails of the last priest." Regarding our present political and cultural state, Diderot, with remarkable prescience, also said, "Those who fear facts will forever try to discredit the fact-finders." On many facets Eisenhower restated Diderot's perspective two hundred years later, lamenting the human inability to progress philosophically, both in mind and in heart.

***

One of Gene Roddenberry's essential facets when developing *Star Trek* in the mid-1960s was the assumption that humanity would evolve with purpose, that what had been hoped for after the Great War, and even more so after World War II, had come to be in the twenty-third century. What he would depict in his series would not be possible, he posited, until the foibles of homo sapiens had been conquered – irrationality, subjectivism, tribalism, and discrimination in general, particularly racism and sexism. As well, dealing with and overcoming not only lack of imagination, but also failure of imagination. Today, more than fifty years on, Rodenberry's science fiction remains just that – fiction. And today we find Diderot's quotes as true as ever, as are Eisenhower's.

Although the 1950s vision of human spaceflight reflected and depicted in *Collier's* and by Walt Disney was a very American view, as well as a somewhat more realistic view regarding the technology of the day, the serious notion of space travel had emerged after World War I, however technologically unattainable it was at the time.

David Lasser, an American political activist and a science fiction writer, published *Conquest of Space* in 1931. The book was partly science fiction, in that an imagined but realistic journey to the moon was told. The other part, however, the primary part, was a straightforward, detailed account of rocket science and technology of the day.

The next year the book caught the attention of fourteen-year-old Archie Clarke, whom the world would later know as Arthur C. Clarke. Based on the cover, the young Clarke thought the book was an adventure story in space, the sort of book he'd often read before. Such wild tales beyond Earth had been around for decades. Quoting from the excellent book *Chasing the Moon*, by Robert Stone and Alan Andres, "Until that moment Archie had assumed space travel was a fantasy. Now he learned that it was actually possible for humans to leave their planet and explore space and that it could happen in the not-too-distant future." Continuing, "In the early 1930s, few in government, media, or business regarded human spaceflight as a serious possibility. But in Archie Clarke's mind it held transforming and liberating options. If the human species could escape the confines of gravity, was it conceivable that other fantastic possibilities might come to pass in the near future as well?" In other words, what if one group of humans demonstrated to all other humans that the impossible ... isn't?

Roddenberry was essentially restating what dreamers such as Tsiolkovsky and Goddard – what all dreamers looking heavenward – both hoped and cautiously assumed. That such a path, such a deliberate path, would change the course of human dynamics and cultural evolution for the better. Since before 1900 space travel tales not of fantasy had come from forward-thinking writers. Such tales were told at some level of science fiction; i.e., highly speculative fiction but extrapolated from the technology of the day. Forward-thinking scientists from then lent credence to these visions. The grasp of young Archie Clarke would be shared increasingly by others after World War II, to gain momentum in government and industry into the 1950s, and then more so into the 1960s.

NASA was formed in 1958. The agency evolved out of N.A.C.A., the National Advisory Committee for Aeronautics. (N.A.C.A. is an initialism, not an acronym, as NASA is. When referring to N.A.C.A. each letter is pronounced, rather than saying NACKA).

Formed in 1915, N.A.C.A. was a bastion of conservative engineering headquartered in Hampton Roads, Virginia, itself a bastion of conservative Tidewater tradition. In other words, the N.A.C.A. engineers were meticulous, thorough, and on average not young. And they were slow.

Although N.A.C.A. was absorbed into NASA, geography fomented a split among personnel. At first the change seemed like an uprooting, but it was really a watershed moment that was part of the aforementioned serendipity of Apollo.

Most of the old timers at N.A.C.A. figured manned spaceflight was poppycock, landing on the moon balderdash. As a result the N.A.C.A. (by now NASA) engineers who moved to Houston from Virginia were young. In fact just about everyone who showed up at the Manned Spacecraft Center (now the Johnson Space Center) from far and wide was young. Some very young. They were welcomed by the city of Houston with great enthusiasm. The old fuddy duddies had been left behind. In a very real sense the relative lack of experience of the Apollo people now in Houston was a treasure. They didn't know what they were doing was impossible, so they did it anyway.

And there's the key. Again, in creating Apollo and reaching the program's primary objective, the scientists, engineers, technicians, and managers of Apollo provided irrefutable evidence that the impossible ... isn't.

We have problems today – huge and existential – that loom larger than those that filled in the *why can't we ___?* blank fifty years ago. If nothing else, human population has almost tripled across the last seventy years or so, as has unbridled consumption. Solving our current problems, however, is not so much a question of *why can't we* as *why won't we?* However overbearing the impossible seems today, is the drive and fortitude within us to do it anyway?

Focusing on the most obvious and insistent problem, the concepts of global warming and climate change have existed in hypotheses for over two hundred years, in data-based theory for over one hundred years, and in objective, extrapolatable fact for over sixty years. Just about all we know about global warming today we knew in 1980. Just about all the questions we have today we had in 1980. In 1980 we knew the steps we needed to take. But we didn't. And we won't, even as we have undeniable evidence the impossible isn't.

The question at hand, then, is just what effect might a continuing and expanding human presence beyond Earth have had on humanity? By the sheer audacity and mere existence of such abilities might we have been able to transcend the seminal, primal traits and fears of human beings? As famed entomologist E.O. Wilson noted about twenty-first century humans, "The real problem of humanity is the following: We have Paleolithic emotions, medieval institutions and godlike technology. And it is terrifically dangerous, and it is now approaching a point of crisis overall."

Newton Minnow, the Federal Communications Commission chairman under Kennedy, implored television network executives to use the technology for the mighty educational tool it could be. On May 9, 1961, he delivered a speech to the National Association of Broadcasters. In his speech he said, "When television is good, nothing – not the theater, not the magazines or newspapers – nothing is better. But when television is bad, nothing is worse. I invite each of you to sit down in front of your television set when your station goes on the air and stay there for a day without a book, without a magazine, without a newspaper, without a profit and loss sheet or a rating book to distract you. Keep your eyes glued to that set until the station signs off. I can assure you that what you will observe is a vast wasteland." From that day forward Minnow was identified by his *vast wasteland* term, at times to his regret.

During World War II Minnow enlisted in the Army at age seventeen, serving his hitch in the Pacific theater. The experience forced Minnow to grow up very fast, leaving him with a longing to improve the world.

Kennedy described himself as "an idealist without illusions." Minnow saw himself in the same light. He held high hopes that television would help create a truly informed citizenry. To that effect, Minnow promoted Telstar to the Kennedy administration and to Congress, and did so vigorously.

Telstar, the first communications satellite, was being developed by AT&T. Typically overlooked as part of the space race, communications satellites was the one area in which the United States was completely ahead of the Soviets. Minnow saw great potential in such satellites to link the world together peacefully and progressively.

The context in which Minnow gave his speech at the broadcaster's meeting, and in which he was foreseeing instant international communication, only amplified the need for his vision. At the time Minnow was making his hopes known *Mr. Ed* premiered on CBS. Mr. Ed was a talking horse, played by Bamboo Harvester, an American Saddlebred. Bamboo Harvester was trained to move his lips on cue to mimic the lines spoken by Allan Lane. Yuks were provided by a laugh track. A few years later *My Mother the Car* made the TV scene on NBC. In the basic plot a man's mother is reincarnated as a car. The two communicate through the car's radio. Mother was played by a 1928 Porter, her voice provided by Ann Sothern. And the yuks were added in postproduction.

Today, sixty years after Minnow's proclaimed hopes, ex-lovers flap their dirty laundry happily on air. Television judges deliver their snarky opinions and verdicts on Hollywood sound stages. Cornhole tournaments are televised, for Pete's sake. Minnow was hardly the first person with a noble vision to be disappointed.

As Minnow writes in his 1995 book *Abandoned in the Wasteland*, in the early 1980s the FCC all but abdicated responsibility for meaningful, educationally dynamic children's programming, which at one time commercial television did produce. The FCC yielded to the lobbying of commercial broadcast and cable television executives in order to turn children into young consumers. This eventual outcome, of course, bore no resemblance to the tool Minnow hoped television might become in the Space Age, in the New Frontier.

In July of 1960, John Kennedy received the nomination to be the presidential candidate of the Democratic party. In one key portion of his acceptance speech he states, "We stand today on the edge of a New Frontier – the frontier of the 1960s, the frontier of unknown opportunities and perils, the frontier of unfilled hopes and unfilled threats."

In later lines he said:

- "Beyond that frontier are uncharted areas of science and space, unsolved problems of peace and war, unconquered problems of ignorance and prejudice, unanswered questions of poverty and surplus."

- "I'm asking each of you to be pioneers towards that New Frontier. My call is to the young in heart, regardless of age."

- "Can we carry through in an age where we will witness not only new breakthroughs in weapons of destruction, but also a race for the mastery of the sky and the rain ... the far side of space and the inside of men's minds?"

- "All mankind waits upon our decision. A whole world waits to see what we shall do. And we cannot fail that trust, and we cannot fail to try."

Kennedy's vision of this new frontier was broad. It included, among other goals, economic stimuli, labor relations, broadening educational opportunities, healthcare expansion, civil rights, and environmental protection. Although exploring beyond Earth was implied more than stated by Kennedy in his speech, for many Americans the New Frontier was synonymous with space exploration. Probably more than any other one event at the beginning of the 1960s, the realization of upward journeys, the actual leaving of Earth, caught the imaginations of human beings across the globe, and in a very focused, exciting, and inspiring way. Apollo was the emblem of the New Frontier.

The hope of Minnow was also the hope of James Webb – of a populace with enough folks who could think both critically and longitudinally, who might respond progressively and forwardly to the idea, and then the fact, of leaving Earth. From Webb's viewpoint America's space exploration was not in competition with Johnson's Great Society, but would complement the goal if the lessons of managing space-age goals were applied to education, technology, and manufacturing.

AAP, and what would have come after, might have been a fertilized seedbed for human thought. The cost of AAP would have been substantial, of course, but only a fraction of the treasure spent fighting the Vietnam War from the late '60s to 1975, those years to have been the initial buildup of AAP. The overall lunar project between 1960 – 1972 cost about $25 billion. NASA's complete spending during this time was about $50 billion.

Earthrise Photo

On December 21, 1968, Apollo 8 lifted off to begin a circumnavigation flight to the moon. The crew of Frank

Borman, James Lovell, and William Anders gave the people of Earth two Christmas gifts. On Christmas Eve, in lunar orbit, the three astronauts read from the Book of Genesis, verses one through ten, regarding the Biblical version of creation. Frank Borman read the final verses, then concluded with, "And from the crew of Apollo 8, we close with good night, good luck, a Merry Christmas – and God bless all of you, all of you on the good Earth." Although some protested, the complete ecumenicalism of the transmission was clear. The crew's message offered hope and optimism at the end of a year that had seen escalating war, the assassinations of Martin Luther King and Robert Kennedy, and violent protests in the streets of America.

The second gift was *Earthrise,* a full-color photo of a two-thirds phase Earth as seen from lunar orbit, taken by Anders on 70mm film using a Hasselblad 500 EL loaded with Kodak Ektachrome film. The photo had serial number AS08-14-2383, indicating the original photo in the original perspective. What we know as *Earthrise* was created in postproduction.

Earthrise connotes the corollary of moonrise on Earth, but this is not the case. The photo is of Earth coming into view as the Apollo 8 CSM orbited the moon. It is not of an Earthrise that would be seen from the lunar surface, which does not happen in the same way moonrise happens as viewed from the surface of Earth.

To produce *Earthrise* the original image was rotated 95° clockwise to make Earth look as though it were rising above the lunar horizon, as if from that point of view. In the original image Earth is to the left of the moon as the crew orbits. But no matter. *Earthrise* had to be in order to convey to Earth's inhabitants a familiar context, and the depiction of our home as a lonely blue and white and brown and green mudball in the cosmos.

The Apollo 8 astronauts were the first human beings in all the history of humanity to see our home from such a distance, to see planet Earth as just that – a planet. A unique ecosystem of gasses and water and photosynthesis, and life of flora and fauna. The inescapable takeaway at that moment was that every living human being in the universe, minus three, was on that world. The bones of every previous human being were on that world. The view was a true parallax of what is only familiarity to billions, and the complacency and the mendacity that comes from such familiarity. And that is what getting off this rock can do.

Fifty years later to the day, December 24, 2018, Anders said, "We set out to explore the moon and instead discovered Earth." Indeed.

Anders was moved greatly by the experience, gaining right then and there that parallax. On that anniversary day Anders also said, "It really undercut my religious beliefs. The idea that things rotate around the pope and up there is a big supercomputer wondering whether Billy was a good boy yesterday? It doesn't make any sense. I became a big buddy of Richard Dawkins."

Wow!

Twenty-four Apollo astronauts went to the moon. All orbited, twelve landed. Although a sense of awe surely entered the consciousness and imagination of all twenty-four to varying degrees and durations, not all were as affected as Anders.

The response among Apollo astronauts ran a spectrum, from simply an assignment to train for and carry out dutifully to the awe and wonder and perplexing questions Anders experienced. Two other Apollo astronauts in particular also experienced life-altering insights during their flights.

Alan Bean was the LM pilot on Apollo 12, and flew the final Skylab mission. Bean resigned from NASA in 1981, becoming an accomplished and highly recognized painter. He had seen sights no artist's eye had ever seen, again in all the history of humanity. He felt compelled and obliged to share his vision with us all, to put this one human being's interpretation on canvas. "I'm the only one who can paint the moon," he told, "because I'm the only one who knows whether that's right or not."

In a quest for accuracy, Bean wanted to add color to the moon, explaining that within the lunar surface are shades of colors. It is not simply gray. "I had to figure out a way to add color to the moon without ruining it," Bean explained. "If I were a scientist painting the moon I would paint it gray. I'm an artist, so I can add colors to the moon."

Edgar Mitchell was the LM pilot for Apollo 14, his only space flight. Reflecting on his view of Earth from the moon he said, "You develop an instant global consciousness, a people orientation, an intense dissatisfaction with the state of the world, and a compulsion to do something about it. From out there on the moon international politics look so petty. You want to grab a politician by the scruff of the neck and drag him a quarter of a million miles out and say, 'Look at that, you son of a bitch.' "

During the return flight to Earth, Mitchell experienced a spontaneous and intense meditative state. In 1973, in Palo Alto, he founded the Institute of Noetic Sciences. The institute studies consciousness and related phenomena. Later in life Mitchell remarked, "So here we are, in the twenty-first century, trying to put two faces of reality – the existence face and the intelligence or conscious face – into the same understanding. Body and mind, physicality and consciousness belong to the same side of reality."

Mitchell was different from Anders and Bean, in that early on – if subconsciously – he had pursued a unification of Western duality, and saw space flight as a way. Later in life he remarked about being drawn to the space program. "After Kennedy announced the moon program, that's what I wanted, because it was the bear going over the mountain to see what he could see, and what could you learn, and I've been devoted to that, to exploration, education, and discovery since my earliest years, and that's what kept me going."

Keep in mind that Anders, Bean, and Mitchell were all fighter jocks, men with the right stuff. And yet intense training, discipline, and dedication to task – inventions of humans – were eclipsed by the utter truth of seeing Earth in its wholly natural state, in a state so unpolitical, so undivided by cultural pettiness.

In Joseph Campbell's *Myths to Live By* is his essay "The Moon Walk – the Outward Journey," written in 1970. This essay is one of the best I've ever read about Apollo 11. In the essay Campbell references a photo of Italian poet Giuseppe

Ungaretti. In the photo the poet is pointing at his television showing Armstrong and Aldrin walking on the moon. The caption told his spellbound words – *Questa è una notte diversa da ogni altra notte del mondo*. (This is a different night from all other nights of the world.)

And indeed it was. And perhaps Signore Ungaretti thus provided the divide among us that defined those who gave momentary notice to Apollo (or those who simply shrugged without giving any notice), and those fewer of us who observed what had been accomplished with a smile – perhaps a laugh out loud – and unbounded wonder and a sense of *Yes, this is important. Just how might not be clear right now, but this is a manifestation of humanity moving ahead.*

That a poet encapsulated the event and caught Campbell's attention is not surprising. At the end of the day, what is $e=mc^2$, really, but poetry? What is the double DNA helix, but poetry? What is the heliocentric solar system, but poetry? Truly, is there any surprise in the notion that Einstein, Crick and Watson, and Copernicus were, somewhere inside, poets? Again quoting E. O. Wilson, "The most successful scientist thinks like a poet – wide-ranging, sometimes fantastical – and works like a bookkeeper. It is the latter role that the world sees."

Anthropologist Margaret Mead understood the poetry in *Earthrise*, saying this one photo justified the entire spending on Apollo. There, hanging in space, was, in fact and indeed, in metaphor and in literalness, Spaceship Earth.

As Campbell notes in his essay, dismissive indifference among the intelligentsia of the day regarding Apollo was typically de rigueur, poetics be damned. In league with rabblerouser Mead, however, was Walter Cronkite, chief CBS news anchor during Apollo. While some of his colleagues often seemed indifferent to Apollo – it was simply news, after all – and even questioned the validity of the program, Cronkite let his inner poet show without restraint or apology, on air, to the nation and the world. With glee and delight and a few tears he let the boy poet inside emerge, and he didn't care. For anyone who didn't like Cronkite's response, that was their problem.

And maybe, more than science, that would have been the purpose of the Apollo Applications Program – discovery, in the broadest and deepest sense for us all. To bring out the poet in enough of us in order for those post-war hopes and dreams of the Great War and then World War II to be possible. To leave behind *the way it's always been, the way it just is, the way it's going to be.* Those words have, across history, comprised the answers from those who refuse to think and imagine, from those who refuse to question their emotional ties to cultural inertia. Who refuse to unleash themselves from overbearing tradition, Diderot's hope. And to prove William Faulkner wrong. In his novel *Requiem for a Nun* he wrote, "The past is never dead. It's not even past."

Poets are not fascists. Poets are not blind followers. Poets are not satisfied with the imagination from others only.

Poets indeed. Alan Bean's stanzas were found in the brush strokes on his canvases. Since he was a young boy Edgar Mitchell had sought the poetry found in the longer view, the distant view, the view of the bear going over the mountain to see what he could see.

Objectively, Project Apollo was, in many ways, more of a reaction than a response. Or perhaps Apollo was a long-anticipated response taking advantage of a reactive point in history. Apollo grew from an intersection of geopolitical and cultural vectors – the Cold War, the post-war years and the New Frontier, and from fundamentally opposed social and economic practices. Perhaps most important, if least defined, from a hunger among many to break profoundly from the past. To date that break has not happened much, certainly not with the profundity Anders or Mitchell or Bean experienced. For the majority of humans such a break has not happened at all.

Earl Hubbard was an influential American artist in the latter half of the twentieth century, creating in the pop style, more or less. In 1969 he published *The Search Is On*. In his book, he posited that the future of humanity, indeed the ultimate survival of humanity, lies beyond our planet. He saw such exploration as truly transcendent, allowing us to evolve to a state in which each of us, as individuals, would be in service to all. He wrote, "The urge to transcend, without a concrete frontier, represents energy without an outlet."

Hubbard uses the word *hygienic* when referring to the states of the planet and of humans living on, and with, the planet. His use is a precursor to the Gaia hypothesis of Earth put forth by Lovelock and Margulis in the mid '70s, which holds that living organisms interact with their inorganic surroundings to form a synergistic, self-regulating system conducive to continuing such life. Hubbard's take was somewhat narrower, referring to the whole of humanity as a single body, one in which an infection, both literally and metaphorically, within a distant culture on a distant land will today affect us all. The passage reads, "There is no challenge on Earth for which we do not possess the means of solution. Man may lack the *will* to respond to the hygienic needs of Mankind, but he does not lack the *means* of solving these hygienic problems. All Earthly problems are hygienic. Earth now represents the body of man, no longer the spirit of man. The urge to transcend is turning our attention out towards the universe. As we seek the means of moving out, we may summon the will to solve the hygienic problems of this body." Hubbard died in 2003. His words from 1969 are hauntingly prescient, for our hygienic state today is deplorable, and we have so far demonstrated the inability to muster the fortitude to implement the solutions we know exist.

The crux of Hubbard's book regards the self-aware state of humans, a state both a gift and, at times, a bane. We alone among creation recognize, and acknowledge, The Future. We alone possess the imagination to wrought The Future, to conceive of the tools needed to realize The Future. We alone possess hands delicate enough to create those tools, and then to drag The Future into existence.

We have the means to address the problems of our shared hygiene. Today, more than ever, we lack the will to act. Like utter fools we have allowed ourselves to be divided into warring tribes by the power hungry and the power mad, by the merely greedy and the astronomically greedy. Allowed? Not the right word, really, since we willingly, happily, and with complicity delivered ourselves to this current state of political and cultural pigeonholing, and to enslavement by 1s and 0s.

Implicit to self-awareness, utterly, is dynamism, which is to say non-stasis. The human state cannot remain healthy – hygienic – standing still. Across history the reach for apotheosis, for that final inviolable state, has failed. Every utopia really does contain its own dystopia, simply because once apotheosis is reached, it must then be enforced. Enforced benevolently and implicitly. Or not, typically. Whereas that enforcement was once not achievable totally by the efforts of analog man, today such enforcement is increasingly achievable in a digital world using AI. That such state is not the right stuff of poets. That such state will find us as clockwork oranges. Not only will we not be wholes greater than our sums, our wholes will be less than our sums.

The original question emerging from human sentience and self-awareness was *How did this happen?* That primal question was followed, almost immediately, one would think, by *What does this mean?* Three hundred thousand years later we still struggle with those questions, most of us far more than a few others. The first question will likely never be answered completely objectively. The second seems more addressable. As Carl Sagan said, "We give our lives meaning by the breadth of our questions and the depth of our answers." Rush drummer Neil Pert had a concise take on existence. In the song "Roll the Bones" he wrote, "Why are we here? Because we're here." Although Pert's question and answer are annoyingly unacceptable to the far more, the few others are fine with them.

Answering our existential questions with myth, superstition, tribalism, and fairytales is easy enough. But in that ease objectivity is lost amid questions not so broad and answers not deep. *How did this happen?* requires an answer, ultimately, that is self-presenting, that needs no interpretation, that does not respond to being evaluated and judged by a person in a position of subjective, unwarranted authority. Considering that *How did this happen?* is likely unanswerable, we are left with the notion that continuing to ask the question is the actual point. Perhaps asking the question is synonymous with exploration, with being a poet.

On May 29, 1953, Edmund Hillary and Tenzing Norgay became the first two humans confirmed to reach the peak of Mount Everest. When asked why he made the climb Hillary gave his famous answer, "Because it's there." His answer was not flippant or dismissive. It was his honest answer. In the simplicity of his answer was profundity. He was Edgar Mitchell's bear going over the mountain to see what he could see.

So, once again, why leave this rock? Why not contain our efforts and treasure to this rock, addressing the hygiene not only of humanity, but also of Gaia? Wouldn't that be exploration, of a sort? Yes it would be, but then exploration followed by a qualifier isn't so much the point.

What Kennedy proposed in the New Frontier, and specifically what was connoted by Apollo as an open-ended project, is found in his September 12, 1962 speech at Rice University. He explained we choose to go to the moon "... because that goal will serve to organize the best of our energies and skills...." Clearly he meant those new skills were to be applied broadly, beyond the space race at the moment and space exploration beyond that moment. Within the context of NASA and the aerospace industry the lunar landing goal did indeed organize the best energies and skills. Within the disengaged context of the populace, and of Congress in particular, there wasn't much organizing.

As referenced earlier, in his speech accepting his selection as the Democratic presidential candidate, Kennedy said, "Can we carry through in an age where we will witness not only new breakthroughs in weapons of destruction, but also a race for the mastery of the sky and the rain ... the far side of space and the inside of men's minds?" What a challenge, then, of vision and courage and fortitude and integrity – to master the far side of space and an understanding of the inside of our minds. It was a challenge we have not met, and, in direct point of fact, are not meeting. Nor is there much indication we soon will meet this challenge.

Returning again to the basic premise at hand, then, would the continuation of Apollo through AAP, and what might have followed, have brought the New Frontier not only into fruition, but into continuing fruition? Would AAP have been seminal in charting not only the far side of space, but, just as important, the inside of our minds? Does the achieving of a goal simply because it is there – in its utter audacity, in its blasphemous breaking of the chains of mindless tradition, in its demonstration that the impossible isn't – bring us as the collective bear to the mountaintop to see what we can see? Those answers, of course, we will never know regarding AAP.

Still, in both hindsight and foresight, just what is to be seen by going over the mountain? Only a previously *un*seen, *un*known frontier in the outward journey, a trek teeming with discovery and opportunity. Only a new perspective, yielding a genuine parallax shift of one's own life and culture as we view the Village of Man lying below in an entirely new and better way, in way previously unknown, previously unimagined. No wonder Astronaut Mitchell wanted to drag any self-serving politician into lunar orbit to observe Earthrise and say, "Look at that, you son of a bitch."

BEYOND 17: THE APOLLO APPLICATIONS PROGRAM AND LOSING THE NEW FRONTIER

In the previous paragraphs are many linguistic variables – might have, could have, perhaps, maybe. Again, we can never know if AAP would have helped realize the hopes of John Kennedy, Newton Minnow, and James Webb, among many others who were their contemporaries. Among many others across the history of rocketry, the Tsiolkovskys and the Goddards. Given that the majority of Americans in 1972 preferred daytime television over live images broadcast from the moon, there was, quite frankly, not much to indicate such realizations would have taken hold.

Today we can only wonder. Had Apollo remained a priority in Congress and the White House, if those leaders had led eagerly and with vision and commitment, perhaps an active engagement with manned space exploration among the populace – with leaving this rock – would have been fostered. There was at least a decent chance whatever path our Space Age world might have taken would have delivered a better world than we now have.

Today we live in a world that has seen a reemergence of religious fundamentalism, tribalism, racism, nationalism, xenophobia, and fascism and general totalitarianism, all amid cascading environmental degradation. Many hundreds of millions, lacking critical and longitudinal thinking skills, believe absurd conspiracy theories. Reality is questioned frequently, to the extent that even the most basic cause-and-effect evidence is denied. Orwellian tendencies that have always been human foibles have been exploited increasingly by self-aggrandized leaders interested only in power and wealth. In the full vision of Orwell, this exploitation is designed to hide itself, designed to create the illusion of original thought.

Our digital life and the looming prospect of a metaverse was science fiction in 1961. Now, rather than outer space, inner space is increasingly becoming our focus. Ironically, the metaverse will offer synthetic experiences of space travel, both fantastic and realistic, delivered to individuals sitting on their couches. Increasingly, we will purchase the imaginations of others rather than cultivate our own imaginations. This is not the right stuff of poets.

An engaged populace might have expected, and demanded, the saga of a continuing and expanding space exploration program. An engaged populace might not have surrendered to the spell of shiny things, of bling. Might not have surrendered to tribalism as visceral, lizard-brain entertainment. Apollo demonstrated that the impossible isn't, after all, and a continuing demonstration might have cohered us, maybe enough of us, into those Roddenberry dreamers from way back.

Perhaps Kennedy envisioned the 1960s as a time when the hopes and dreams after World War I and then again after World War II could be realized. Presently, however, we must acknowledge that our reach has far exceeded our grasp. We must also acknowledge that the weakness of our grasp is our own doing by our own choice. After all, we are the only lifeform on Earth that not only recognizes The Future, but has the imaginative and physical abilities to shape that future.

The previous sentence requires a qualifier, of course, namely that we can shape that future for better, or for worse. And so these questions: What elements and components and viewpoints and philosophies must be in a culture – implicitly more than explicitly, eventually – to bring about *for better*? How do we go about exercising our grasp so it can one day equal our reach, and then one day exceed our reach?

In *2001: A Space Odyssey*, Stanley Kubrick and Arthur Clarke presented a tribe of early hominids. The leader of the tribe is Moonwatcher. Moonwatcher's tribe battles another tribe for territory and food. The give and take between the two tribes is cyclical to the point of deadlock.

In a seminal moment Moonwatcher picks up a bone about three feet long. He discovers very quickly he can use the bone to injure rivals and fend them off. He discovers further he can wield the bone to take down a large animal, bringing to his tribe a level of food security it has never known. This sequence in the film is, of course, Kubrick's metaphor for the beginning of technology, for the beginning of creative intelligence (or intelligent creativity, take your pick) and the self-awareness implicit to such intelligence. The sequence also acknowledges the break of homo sapiens from the natural world.

With his bone as a tool Moonwatcher extends not only his reach, but he also increases the force of the blow by not only the rigidity of the material (compared to his own fist) but also the increased mass of the material, and the increased momentum gained from the longer arc of movement of that mass.

At the very end of the film, main character Astronaut Bowman evolves, by the same alien-provided catalyst that sparked Moonwatcher's insight about the bone, into an embryonic being who is now beyond homo sapiens. And so Kubrick poses the question: Once technology begins, does it end? Implicit to the beginning of technology is the notion that there is no end to technology, although it can be ended explicitly in pursuit of that apotheosis, by choice and definition. This unending aspect is, understandably, unsettling to many. With not much assessment it's fairly obvious that the meaningful application of technology has never been discussed beyond academic and esoteric realms. Historically, the application of technology has in no way always been *for better*. And of course technology can end itself, by the destruction much of technology is designed to deliver.

With technology humans become something more than human. Moonwatcher was more than his tribe mates when he held the bone. Later on, a human riding a horse was, while on the horse, something beyond human. Then later still while driving a car, while flying an airplane, or simply pedaling a bicycle. While looking through a microscope or a telescope. While using a camera or sending a telegram or talking on a telephone. Or living on the moon.

Maybe these technological states of being more than human is what being human is, ultimately. Of all lifeforms on Earth only humans are not genetically sentenced to that apotheosis, however relative that word is within the context of evolution. Evolution, of course, is not at all limited to homo sapiens, and yet the higher apes and cetaceans, which clearly have some level of intelligence and an ability to learn, and possibly some self-awareness, seem to have reached a relative end point. Again, within the context of evolution, that endpoint is not static. However, set against the changes in pre-human hominids leading to us, other higher species change in very slow motion. Dolphins, for example, are part of cetacean evolution that began fifty million years ago with land mammals, and yet dolphins have not changed in millions of years. Three hundred thousand years ago, a blink in geologic and evolutionary time, homo sapiens did not exist, and yet now we do.

Maybe the answer to why leave this rock, then, is simply because we can, and because in creating the ability to leave we learn about ourselves and about the inside of our minds, with a breadth and a depth as yet not known. In so doing we would organize the best of our energies and skills. We would once again find out that the impossible isn't, which might give us the insight and the impetus to bring about *for better* across the entire human spectrum, indeed for all of creation.

Part of that organizing in pursuit of *for better,* and of learning about ourselves and the inside of our minds, must, without fail, be an awareness of our environmental impact on another world, and managing that impact, even if that other world is deemed lifeless. In addition, the active non-militarization of where we might go is paramount. Of course, stating what I just stated is easy, simply pressing the right letters on a keyboard. Actually pulling off those goals would go a long way towards Roddenberry's vision, towards pursuing *for better,* towards learning more about ourselves than we ever have, towards achieving that interior mental survey, towards organizing our best efforts.

***

This book began with John Kennedy. It ends – appropriately, somewhat ironically – with Lyndon Johnson. The two men, from very different backgrounds, were quite unalike.

Kennedy was a handsome man, an Eastern patrician, a product of prep schools, a graduate of Harvard. Johnson was born in a Stonewall, Texas farmhouse, eventually graduating from the Southwest Texas State Teachers College. Jug-eared as a boy, he would grow to have a practical face as a man. Although Johnson always appeared a generation older than Kennedy, the two were just nine years apart.

Whereas Kennedy's vision of a New Frontier was rooted to a degree in his privilege, and the broad socioeconomic assumptions that can come from such ease, Johnson had witnessed, and sometimes lived, hardscrabble accomplishment. More to the point, he learned how to hold on to such accomplishment, plant his feet in it, and then move ahead. Initially Kennedy's vice president, Johnson succeeded to the presidency after Kennedy's assassination, then was elected president in his own right in 1964.

Political ambitions were evident in Johnson as a young teenager. He entered politics formally in 1931 as the legislative secretary to Texas Representative Richard Kleberg. Kleberg left the daily responsibilities of being a Congressman largely up to Johnson, allowing Johnson the opportunity to learn early on the nuts-and-bolts of the backside of politics. By the time Johnson was elected to the House in 1937, at age twenty-eight, he was a skilled politician. He was elected to the Senate in 1948, resigning his seat in 1961 to become vice president, all along the way honing his observations of people, and so his political skills.

Within those skills was the arm twisting for which Johnson was famous. Or reviled. He had a keen knack for reading people, and for discerning their weaknesses and their hopes. In larger scope he applied this ability to groups, to states, to regions, to the entire nation.

Johnson's role in Apollo was less transparent than Kennedy's, but certainly no less important. While Kennedy used the power and prestige of his office to take the political leap that would lead to Armstrong's giant leap, Johnson once again dealt with the machinations of the situation – the planning and execution of Apollo, the politics involved.

On the night of the day Sputnik was launched Johnson was at his ranch in Texas. His wife, Lady Bird, recalls the two of them looking up into a clear sky. "We had lived with the sky all our lives," she recalled, "and suddenly it was as though we had never seen it before. That was our launching pad, so to speak."

Indeed it was. Back at the ranch house Johnson began making phone calls. Before that day was over he had received approval to begin the *Inquiry into Satellite and Missile Program.* The findings of the inquiry led to direct action regarding expanding U.S. space activity.

While Eisenhower and Congress were concerned about offensive Soviet missiles and national security, as was Johnson, Johnson was convinced a broader pursuit of space exploration would produce results beneficial to all of America. In his Great Society speech, delivered at the University of Michigan in May of 1964, he asked Americans, "Will you join in the battle to build the Great Society, to prove that our material progress is only the foundation on which we will build a richer life of mind and spirit?" Very likely Johnson was riffing off Kennedy's

New Frontier speech, in which, to recall, Kennedy said, "But the New Frontier of which I speak is not a set of promises – but a set of challenges. It sums up not what I intend to *offer* the American people, but what I intend to *ask* of them." As well, Johnson was certainly remembering his predecessor's question to the American people (referencing it yet once again), "Can we carry through in an age where we will witness not only new breakthroughs in weapons of destruction, but also a race for the mastery of the sky and the rain ... the far side of space and the inside of men's minds?" For more than fifty years now history has shown our collective answer to both questions has been *no*.

After that Sputnik night Johnson urged Eisenhower to create NASA, replacing the mired N.A.C.A. In very many ways Lyndon Johnson *was* the start of Apollo. Quoting historian Andreas Reichstein, "All actions of Congress with regard to space between 1957 and 1961 can be attributed to Johnson."

What would become the Apollo Applications Program was begun by Johnson in early 1964, when he summoned James Webb, asking him to lay out future missions that would take advantage of existing or scheduled Apollo hardware.

In December of 1968, the White House hosted a formal dinner to present the Medal of Freedom to Webb, who had resigned as Administrator of NASA two months earlier.[15] The dinner was also a tribute to all astronauts, in particular Frank Borman, Jim Lovell, and Bill Anders, in attendance that night, who would launch on Apollo 8 not two weeks later.

Wally Schirra spoke at the dinner, the only astronaut doing so. The undercurrent of the night was the fate of Apollo, the budget cuts to the program already made. A new administration, a Republican administration, would take power in just a few weeks, leaving Apollo in the hands of Richard Nixon.

A number of months earlier Johnson visited the Michoud Assembly Facility in Louisiana, where Chrysler was building the first stages of the Saturn I and the Saturn IB, and where Boeing would build the Saturn V first stage.

Talk of layoffs abounded among the employees. Johnson was there to deliver a speech, to offer hope and encouragement. Schirra was also there. In a private moment Johnson took Schirra aside. "It's unfortunate," Johnson began, "but the way the American people are, now that they have developed all of this capability, instead of taking advantage of it, they'll probably just piss it all away."

Notes

1. Notions that Apollo was a hoax have existed for decades. Many are based on perceived photographic evidence. Among the most popular examples are:

- The American flag is not only extended from the pole, but appears to be flapping on the airless moon. Explanation: The flag was extended on a spline, which was bent accidentally, rippling the fabric.

- No stars are visible in photographs taken on the lunar surface. Explanation: The lunar surface is highly reflective. To avoid overexposure the cameras were set at from $1/150^{th}$ to $1/250^{th}$ of a second, far too fast for faint starlight to expose the film.

- A photograph of Aldrin standing on the footpad below the ladder on the lunar module shows him well lit, even though he is in the shadow of the lunar module. Explanation: The sun, Earthlight, and the lunar surface were all light sources, reflecting off the bright white pressure suit.

- A photograph of Aldrin lifting his foot from the regolith shows a sharply defined imprint. Only a substance like wet sand, deniers claim, would be able to maintain the sharp angles made by the imprint of the wide treads on Aldrin's boot. Explanation: Regolith is similar to volcanic ash in texture. It compresses easily into shapes that remain.

- Left behind equipment, including three lunar rovers and six descent stages (plus a crashed descent stage from Apollo 10), are not visible using even the most powerful telescopes. Explanation: These objects are simply beyond the resolution of Earth-based or space-based telescopes. The lunar module would appear as just .15 pixels in the Hubble Space Telescope field of view, literally a very small unidentifiable dot on the lunar surface. In June of 2009 the Lunar Reconnaissance Orbiter was launched. The Orbiter made high resolution images of robotic and human exploration sites showing hardware, the tracks of astronauts and lunar rovers, and disturbances in the regolith from descent and ascent engines.

- In one photograph odd light patterns are seen in the blackness of space, obviously studio lights. Explanation: These are simply lens flares. In the photo is also a pentagonal washed-out area mimicking the aperture itself, a typical result of lens flare. And think about it. Would NASA, having gone to the trouble and expense of this soundstage production, have so cavalierly let such a photo be released?

The van Allen radiation belt is also cited as evidence that Apollo was a hoax. The claim is any astronaut flying through the belt would be fried by radiation. The two basic types of radiation are electromagnetic waves and charged particles, also known as ionizing radiation. Charged particles can compromise the materials of a spacecraft and cause tissue damage in humans if the exposure is intense enough over a long enough time period. Those two variables are key. Similar to a pilot plotting a course around a thunderstorm, the Apollo command module took a course avoiding the inner belt, the most lethal part, moving instead through the thinnest parts of the outer belt. In both coming and going, Apollo astronauts spent a combined total of three hours exposed to the belt.

Photographs are just one facet from a catalog of faked moon landing evidence that has emerged over more than fifty years. Within this catalog are such notions that claim Apollo was faked to divert public attention from the Vietnam war, and that Stanley Kubrick directed the scenes.

Finally, in the larger scope, does anyone truly think the Soviets would not have jumped on any genuine evidence that Apollo had been faked?

2. In 1972 television was broadcast by the three commercial networks, and the fledgling PBS. Cable systems were simply local operations that captured broadcast signals at a central antenna, then routed those signals along coaxial cables to remote areas beyond the broadcast reach. There was no home satellite television or twenty-four-hour news. News from the field was gathered on 16mm film. Streaming was what rivers and creeks did.

3. Live television transmission from the moon is an unsung achievement. The imaging abilities of smart phones, and the instant distribution available through the internet, were unimagined in 1962, when television specifications for the Apollo missions were defined. In 1962 GoPro could have been the name of a golf club, or maybe even a dog food, but not the name of small remote video cameras transmitting to Wi-Fi.

Digital transmission was considered for Apollo, but the technology was still under development, using too much band width. As well, CCD technology was in its early days. As a result, analog signals were transmitted from the moon to the CM, then relayed to Earth across 240,000 miles. The television cameras used standard vidicon tubes, which were fragile. All components in the cameras had to withstand a 500-degree Fahrenheit temperature range, from -250° to 250° (-157° C to 121° C).

The first black-and-white transmissions used a slow scanning system. Those images had to be converted to standard television specifications of the day. The signals on all missions, but especially color signals, were subjected to the Doppler effect, also requiring technical corrections. Other technical anomalies unique to Apollo applications required compensating for the signal – essentially cleaning it up – once the signal was received at Earth stations. From the initial lunar surface transmissions to the resulting images on home televisions the process was completely analog. The initial camera image was crude even for the times. By the time images reached the home viewer the original image was significantly degraded, due to the compensating and manipulation, and to extended analog transmission by satellite and microwave relay that increased signal noise. By Apollo 17 the images had improved significantly.

Both RCA and Westinghouse manufactured the cameras. In general RCA manufactured the black-and-white cameras used early on, Westinghouse the color cameras used on Apollo 10, and then on all subsequent missions for landing site transmissions. The lunar rover color cameras used on Apollo 15, 16, and 17, controlled remotely from mission control, were made by RCA.

In particular, the Westinghouse color camera was groundbreaking. Although small consumer-level black-and-white television field cameras would be available in the late 1960s, in 1964, when Westinghouse was awarded the contract, color cameras were still large, the size of a dorm refrigerator. They were mounted on massive rolling tripods, were complicated, and power hungry. The Westinghouse color camera was about the size of a shoe box and weighed less than eight pounds.

In 1970 both NASA and Westinghouse received an Emmy Award for outstanding Achievement in Technical/Engineering Development. Westinghouse for designing and fabricating the camera, NASA for its role in defining the technical parameters of the camera.

4. The N1 is typically described as a five-stage rocket. Such a description requires clarification of the three-stage Saturn V.

The first three stages of the Saturn V boosted the command service module (CSM) and the lunar module (LM) into Earth orbit. The CSM consisted of the Apollo capsule attached to a single-engine rocket that would propel the capsule and the LM to the moon, and then propel the capsule back to Earth. On launch the LM was stowed just below the CSM rocket nozzle, in the faring that sloped between the top of the instrument unit (directly above stage three) and the CSM. In Earth orbit the CSM docked with the LM, meaning the LM was attached to the top of the CSM, legs forward, as the combined component, now ungainly looking, journeyed to lunar orbit.

The N1 lunar rocket was known as the N1-23. Stages one, two, and three duplicated the like stages of the Saturn V. The L3 section held one stage for trans-lunar injection (establishing a trajectory from Earth orbit to the moon), as well as a second stage to carry the LK lander to the lunar surface, as well as to propel the Soyuz 7K-LOK spacecraft back to Earth.

From this point of view, then, the Saturn V system actually had four stages, the CSM being the fourth.

5. The Soviets did beat the U.S. regarding lunar flight on one facet. Zond 5 was launched September 14, 1968, more

than three months before Apollo 8, which flew three astronauts to the moon, orbiting ten times before returning to Earth. Zond 5 was an altered Soyuz spacecraft. The Soyuz capsule with related components was the equivalent of the CSM and LM configuration.

The Soviet's original intention was to have Zond 5 be a crewed mission, thus being the first to transport humans to the moon (but not land). However, Zond missions 1 – 3 were failures. Zond 4 was only a partial success, and so the Soviets were very reluctant to risk cosmonauts on Zond 5.

Zond 5 was the first spacecraft to reach the moon in a flyby (it did not orbit), the first lunar craft to return safely to Earth, and the first to take lifeforms to the vicinity of the moon, including two tortoises and assorted plants.

At the time of launch, and of course earlier when a crewed Zond 5 mission was considered, the Soviets could not have known of Apollo 8, which didn't emerge as an idea until August. Apollo 8 was originally to have been a test of the CSM and the LM in Earth orbit in early 1969, but the LM was not ready. In the interest of flight continuity the revised Apollo 8 mission was hatched. The Earth-orbit test was reassigned to Apollo 9.

As of late 1968 that the first lunar landing might be made by cosmonauts was still seen as a real possibility at NASA, but not by the Soviets, who knew by this date the race was lost. The CIA, using various radio dishes around the world, monitored Soviet space communications routinely. They were using the Jodrell Bank Observatory in England during the Zond 5 mission.

To yank NASA's chain a group of cosmonauts arranged to have their voices transmitted to the Zond 5 spacecraft, which then relayed the transmissions back to Earth. The three read telemetry data, and began to discuss landing procedures. Later, cosmonaut Pavel Popov took the microphone at the control center in Crimea and said, "The flight is proceeding according to normal, we're approaching the surface." The prank worked. Eugene Cernan, of Apollo 17, said the incident "shocked the hell out of us."

6. Ballooning, not surprisingly, goes back to China around 250 AD, when balloons were used to send military signals. The first recorded hot air balloon carrying passengers rose on November 21, 1783. The first hydrogen balloon carrying passengers rose on December 1, 1783. Both milestones took place in France.

Although ballooning is part of aviation history, it is separate from controlled flight or rocketry. Control is imprecise and secondary to lift. Ballooning is limited by the height of Earth's atmosphere, as, of course, are winged aircraft. Some present-day outfits propose sending tourists to space in a pressurized chamber lifted by balloon, but such an airship could not exceed the Karman line, a somewhat loose boundary between Earth's atmosphere and the vacuum of space. The Karman line is set at 100 kilometers, or 62 miles.

7. In 1953 The Viking Press published *Conquest of the Moon*. The book was written by Wernher von Braun, Fred L. Whipple, and Willy Ley, edited by Ryan. Within the book is a concise presentation of how to travel from the Earth to the moon. Although the pages contain a technological and

funding hopefulness from that time, often extreme, they contain no science fiction.

In the text, and within the illustrations, diagrams, and charts, is a fully thought out, precise method of realizing the different components of a moon journey from the technological perspective of the time. The building of the space station, the design of the space vehicles and constructing them in orbit at the station, the method of landing cargo and crew on the moon, establishing a lunar base, and exploring the moon. Although written for a popular audience, and containing speculative and untested designs, the text is not specious. The authors present a serious proposal of some scientific and technological depth.

Remarkable is that this proposal is from seventy years ago. Seventy years ago the mathematics of rocketry, orbital mechanics, and a lunar journey was long known. What a rocket to the moon would look like was known. (Due to the fact that rockets constructed in orbit would never travel in atmosphere, the 1953 rockets looked nothing like Apollo.) The level of consumables for rockets and astronauts – fuel, food, water, and oxygen – was known. The most efficient courses to go to and return from the moon were known. How to generate electricity in space from solar power was known. Quoting from the text, "There are no problems involved to which we don't have the answers – or the ability to find them – today."

Conquest of the Moon reflects an astonishing level of optimism, if at times somewhat reckless, not knowable today. The purpose of the book you're reading now is to illustrate how the 1961 vision of Apollo began to be whittled away nearly from the start. The point of view presented in *Conquest of the Moon* illustrates that by the time the lunar mission that would be Apollo started in earnest, the broad scope of lunar exploration was already scaled down significantly.

8. TWA, founded in 1930, was one of the original Big Four domestic carriers, along with Eastern, American, and United. Howard Hughes gained control of TWA in 1939, expanding flights worldwide. Pan Am, founded in 1927, would become the premier intercontinental carrier. The company pioneered flights across the Pacific by establishing island refueling stations. Pan Am typically led the industry in modern aircraft acquisitions and operations innovations.

Given the forward thinking evident in both TWA and Pan Am, it's no surprise each was linked to future flights beyond the atmosphere, moving from jet engines to rocket engines, in somewhat the same way each airline had moved from piston-driven propeller engines to jet engines. Their intentions were, of course, more wishful than necessarily achievable. Still, a seriousness – or a hopefulness, anyway – was to be found in their gossamer projections.

Eventually Pan Am and TWA both would go the way of AAP. Despite Pan Am's pioneering history establishing long-haul flights across the world and the airline's optimism and enthusiasm, no space clipper was ever built; no Pan Am craft of any sort would ever achieve even sub orbit. The airline closed shop in 1991. TWA would fly no one to the moon, flying no one anywhere after 2001.

9. Returning to Tomorrowland for a moment, Disney designer John Hench knew from the start he would depict the TWA Moonliner fictionally. Hench was a fine artist with a psychological understanding of the masses. For ten years the

public's idea of a rocket had been the V2, and so the Moonliner would reflect the V2 look to take advantage of that subliminal understanding. In other words, show biz. As the public later observed real rockets the Moonliner was refitted to some degree with ersatz details from actual rockets, such as steam outlets to simulate lox burn off.

In 1960, perhaps because Howard Hughes was no longer majority shareholder, TWA withdrew its Moonliner support. Douglas Aerospace stepped in, replacing the TWA logo with its own.

A two-year revamping of Tomorrowland would find the Moonliner removed in 1965, replaced by Rocket Jets. Rather than an exhibit that stimulated imagining The Future among the attendees Rocket Jets was, ironically, clearly nothing more than a theme park ride. In 1971 the Flight to the Moon attraction opened at Disney World in Orlando. By that time the attraction was already dated somewhat, given the reality of Apollo, and therefore anticlimactic. It was replaced by Mission to Mars in 1975, which was pretty much the same deal as Flight to the Moon. Mission to Mars ran until 1993, far more as a *what might have been* exhibit than a *world to come* exhibit.

10. LOR can also mean the lander and the main spacecraft being launched separately, then travelling separately to lunar orbit. Once both were in orbit the lander would dock with the main spacecraft, from which the landing crew would transfer. At the end of the mission the lander would again dock with the main spacecraft, the crew then transferring back.

During the Apollo missions the LM and the CSM docked in Earth orbit, travelling to the moon in that configuration. This method does not diminish the meaning of LOR, since the astronauts returning from the moon docked in lunar orbit with the CSM.

11. Scott Carpenter, Gordon Cooper, John Glenn, Gus Grissom, Wally Schirra, Alan Shepard, Deke Slayton.

12. The next group of astronauts, NASA group 2 (also known as the Next Nine or the New Nine) were Neil Armstrong, Frank Borman, Pete Conrad, Jim Lovell, James McDivitt, Elliot See, Tom Stafford, Ed White, and John Young.

13. Chapter 11 began as a lengthy end note, but I found it expanding and then expanding more. With the order of the original chapters already in sequence I kind of shoehorned this chapter in, which makes it sort of an 800-pound gorilla. But then that's the subject at hand.

14. Herbert George Wells (1866-1946) raised himself up from very little. Highly precocious, at ten he began writing and illustrating stories. From that early age he was interested in The Future, which is to say challenging and changing the stasis of the present day and what had come before.

Even as a child he pushed strongly against the constraints and morés of Victorian England, refusing to accept his prescribed station in life, one dictated by tradition and social class. As an adult he would challenge the idea of sex as nothing more than the biological utility of procreation, and would champion the rights and liberation of women. His views would have been shocking in the 1950s. In the late 1800s they were scandalous.

Wells was a trained zoologist. His scientific background lent credence to his science fiction writing, which included *The Time Machine*, *The Island of Doctor Moreau*, and *The War* *of the World*s, among many other works. He also wrote the well-received *A Short History of the World*. In his day Wells was one of the most widely read writers.

Wells was a genuine futurist. He foretold the coming of tanks, aircraft, space travel, and nuclear weapons. He even envisioned a sort of seminal version of the internet. Considering that he lived the first half of his life in the age of steam, his foresight into The Future was wholly remarkable.

15. On October 7, 1968, President Johnson recommended, but did not specifically ask for, Webb's resignation. Johnson wanted Thomas Paine, NASA's deputy administrator, as acting director when Apollo 7, the first crewed flight, launched four days later. Johnson reasoned if Apollo 7 or 8 experienced a serious mishap, or ended in tragedy, Webb could better serve the program behind the scenes while Paine took the heat.

Sources

Books

Abandoned in the Wasteland – Newton Minnow

Above and Beyond – The Encyclopedia of Aviation and Space Sciences – various authors

Across the Airless Wilds – Earl Swift

Across the Space Frontier – Wernher von Braun, Cornelius Ryan, et alia

Apollo Applications Program Summary Report – NASA

Apollo, The Race to the Moon – Charles Murray and Catherine Bly Cox

Chasing the Moon – Robert Stone and Alan Andres

Conquest of the Moon – Wernher von Braun, Fred L. Whipple, and Willy Ley

Kennedy Space Center, Gateway to Space – David West Reynolds

Myths to Live By – Joseph Campbell

1959 – Fred Kaplan

Saturn Flight Manual – NASA

Space Stations – Roger D. Launius

Stages to Saturn – Roger E. Bilstein

The Right Stuff – Tom Wolfe

The Search is On – Earl Hubbard

This New Ocean: A History of Project Mercury – Lloyd S. Swenson, Jr. and James F. Grimwood

War Is a Racket – Gen. Smedley D. Butler

Wired magazine and David S. F. Portree

Websites

asronautix.com – Mark Wade
  jpl.nasa.gov
  lunar.org
  nasa.gov
  primidi.com
  spaceflighthistories.com
  spaceflighthistory.blogspot.com – David S. F. Portree
  spaceskyrocket.de – Gunter Krebs
  whitehousehistory.org
  wikipedia.org
  wired.com

Also by Fairleigh Brooks

Fiction
Notes of a Would-Be Astronaut

"Exhausted and frustrated by compromise, Tom McAllister hits the highways in search of self. Although reminiscent of Jack Kerouac's *On the Road*, *Notes of a Would-Be Astronaut* is better. This cross-country odyssey is a trip I thoroughly enjoyed."

– Laurie Birnsteel, author of *Sunspot* and *Kahala*

"An engaging inner and outer travelogue, replete with vivid descriptions, vignettes of fascinating characters, and inner knots reminiscent of R.D. Laing. This story of *Passages*-midlife crisis search for self is sure to resonate with many of us, especially those who like to think while they read. Enjoy!"

– Stan Franklin, author of Artificial Minds

Other Fiction

Mr. Willy & Arthur
A Presentation of Short Stories Without Regard to Marketing
Lady Chatterley's Pool Boy

About the Author

Fairleigh Brooks has written about the history of science and technology in numerous articles and commentaries over the years. Being a space cadet since he was a small boy, that interest has focused largely on space exploration, specifically manned space exploration. Within these considerations Brooks has explored how technology arose, its purpose, and how technology changes the ideas and concepts of who we are, and why we are.

Wordsmith on LinkedIn[1]

Topics from space exploration to architecture to civil rights to Charlie Brown's Christmas.

---

1. https://www.linkedin.com/in/fairleigh-brooks-8161b344/recent-activity/shares/

9 798822 374959 2